THE WAR SYSTEM

AND

YOU

INSTITUTE FOR INTERNATIONAL STUDIES
Chapel Hill, North Carolina

THE WAR SYSTEM

AND

YOU

JACK LASLEY

Publisher

INSTITUTE FOR INTERNATIONAL STUDIES

Box 538

CHAPEL HILL, NORTH CAROLINA

U.S.A.

Library of Congress Catalogue Number 65-14419

Copyright, 1965, by the
Institute for International Studies
Box 538, Chapel Hill, North Carolina, USA
Printed in the United States
of America

First Edition

24010

To

The Youth of Today and Tomorrow

The Author

Jack Lasley is the author of numerous articles on the need for the rule of law in international affairs. He is a charter member of the World Law Center, the American Freedom Association, a Counsellor of the Supreme Court of the United States and a member of the National Panel of Arbitrators of the American Arbitration Association.

ACKNOWLEDGMENTS

I gratefully acknowledge my intellectual indebtedness to Grenville Clark, Norman Cousins, Robert Lee Humber, Arthur Larson, Charles S. Rhyne, Louis B. Sohn and to those other great men of vision who have seen the need for a world rule of law.

The tireless typing of Jane Barclay and the sensitive editing of Barbara Reitt are sincerely appreciated.

J. L.

"The formation of an authoritative all-powerful world order is the ultimate aim towards which we must strive. Unless some effective world super-government can be brought quickly into action, the proposals for peace and human progress are dark and doubtful."

—WINSTON CHURCHILL

INTRODUCTION

Since the advent of nuclear weapons, there has been an enormous increase in the threat to nations of uncontrolled national armies. This danger to the survival of nations will increase in the years ahead as the proliferation of these weapons continues. While we cannot indefinitely keep nuclear weapons know-how from nations, we can and must set about the business of bringing national armies and nuclear power under effective universal control. The accomplishment of this end is the concern of all mankind and therefore will require effective international authority.

The present nuclear arms race is in effect a dash along a crumbling roadway on the edge of a chasm that offers not life, liberty, freedom and security, but destruction to all nations and their peoples regardless of their political philosophy.

Yet, nations are fearful of unilateral disarmament. The West fears that such action would result in a worldwide Communist take-over. Communist nations fear that should they disarm, capitalist imperialists would rule the world. There obviously must be a protecting force created to allay these fears and fill the void left as nations deemphasize armaments.

Granting that there are evils in both major contending political philosophies, the greatest evil lies in their mutual approach to national security. Their reciprocal threat of nuclear annihilation must give way in the name of mankind to international security through law and government.

This is not a pacifist preachment, but a call for practical, effective national patriotism in the nuclear age. Force will be needed in a governed world to insure compliance with world law, but force to implement law would be no more than we now witness in our own cities, states and nations throughout the world. Force used at the world level under a rule of law would be with international sanction and in the name of mankind, clearly distinguishable from present lynch-mob unilateral national force which threatens to drag all nations down to destruction in an orgy of nuclear attacks.

Much has been written concerning the movement for civil rights for minority groups. What has been tragically overlooked is that both minority and majority have lost to the war system rights and freedoms far in excess of those that have commanded their chief attention. No man can be free as long as national armies sap the resources of his nation and threaten the destruction of his homeland and his very species.

We must re-examine, then, our traditional concept of patriotism. A willingness to die in battle will no longer suffice in the service of liberty, freedom and defense of country. From an emphasis on death, patriotism should now be measured in terms of life and a vigorous willingness to work for those world-level institutions or arms control which will relieve men and nations from the threat of nuclear destruction. What possible good is effected if we destroy our enemy only to be destroyed ourselves?

What liberty is gained, what freedom served and whose homeland is protected if nations are rent asunder and millions of civilians incinerated? To call for nuclear war in the name of "freedom," "liberty," and "defense of homeland" is to prostitute the true meaning of these treasured terms.

This has been called the "silent" generation because it has failed to produce a vigorous political movement to solve the universal problem posed by the threat of nuclear war. Our great danger lies in a continuation of this silence. Many citizens feel they cannot be individually effective in seeking a solution to the problem of nuclear weaponry. They have, therefore, withdrawn from participation in peace groups because, in addition to feeling that their personal involvement would be futile, they fear such activity might be considered unpatriotic since peace groups de-emphasize military power which has been touted to be the salvation of our nation and its way of life. Yet, our religious principles and our national survival both now direct us to shift our emphasis from nations and war systems to people, and to view world problems with universal perspective rather than from narrow nationalistic viewpoints.

By so doing we can see more clearly the pathway to freedom and national survival in the years ahead; we can see more clearly the interdependence of all men, their sufferings and overpowering burden of misery; we can see more clearly the need to strengthen the world structure of law and order to harness the forces of unbridled national armies. Most fundamentally, we will come to understand that by shifting our emphasis in world affairs from nations to people we can through law and government relieve the moral and financial burden of armaments now pressing down on all nations so that mankind may begin a decisive world-wide war on ignorance, poverty and disease.

This book is addressed to all the people of the earth in the hope that they will awaken to the need for their participation in the quest to substitute the force of law for the law of force in international affairs.

JACK LASLEY

Chapel Hill, North Carolina

CONTENTS

PART V. APPENDIXES

"Who is the slayer, who is the victim? Speak."
— Sophocles

MILITARY DEVICES—
SECURITY OR SUICIDE?

Gas Warfare

Although nuclear weapons are the most widely discussed, they are far from being the only satanic devices in the arsenals of the major powers. Constant research seeks to uncover more effective gases, and disease germs are being cultivated in elaborate government laboratories for deliberate use against people and animals in the event of war.

When the Allies entered Germany during World War II, they found a colorless, almost odorless gas called Tabun. This nerve gas, developed during the final stages of the war by the Germans, attacks the eyes and lungs causing death within one to five minutes. Droplets of Tabun can rapidly penetrate clothing, be absorbed by the skin and bring death within ten minutes to two hours. This gas, previously unknown, is now stored in large quantities in the United States and Russia.

It is interesting to speculate why gas was not used during World War II. First, gas had proven relatively unreliable during World War I. For example, of the 73,000 Americans gassed only 2 per cent died; whereas of the American soldiers receiving other wounds, 20 per cent died. Weather, particularly wind and rain, played a significant role in the use of gas and at times would make its effective use practically impossible. Also during World War II, there was still a residue of the abhorrence to the use of gas that swept the world after the gassings of World War I. Certainly, too, of great significance, is the fact that nuclear weapons were not used until the very last stages of World War II. This introduced an awesome new dimension into warfare that has probably removed any vestige of compunction to the use of gas that may have carried over from the First World War into the pre-atomic period.

We are now developing highly exotic gases. Scientific breakthroughs have made gas a first-line weapon for the next war. Among the significant developments is the advent of the psycho chemicals; those gases that destroy a man's ability to function. Best known are lysergic acid diethylamide (LSD-25), mescaline, and psilocybin. These have been appropriately termed the "madness" gases. They can make strong men weak, timid and languorous and otherwise change a man's character. They attack a man's very personality and make him unresponsive to stimuli. Another group of gases incapacitates men physically and without pain, robbing them of their ability to integrate time and distance; men are temporarily paralyzed, placed in a deep sleep or blinded.

These particular gases render a man as ineffective as if he had been killed, but the effect is generally temporary. Thus, there would be no compunction on the part of the military to use these new gases. It will no doubt be argued by the military that these gases constitute a "humanitarian" approach to war in that their effect is only temporary.

After the cremation of hundreds of thousands of innocent civilians with napalm, phosphorus and finally nuclear bombs during World War II, the military views gas warfare as but another way to demoralize and destroy the enemy. The first gas to be used in the future will probably be one of the non-lethal psycho gases, but once the precedent is set for the use of gas the lethal gases will soon follow.

New lethal gases are now being developed. One is called Sarin, and it is far more powerful than the German gas Tabun found in Germany by the Allies at the close of the war. Sarin causes the muscles of the body to tighten continually. Normal muscle tightening is controlled by a substance in the body called cholinesterase. Sarin blocks the function of the body's cholinesterase so that all the body's muscle systems including those affecting the vital organs continue to tighten by acetylccholine action into rigid paralysis. Sarin can be delivered by shell, bomb, rocket or by spraying. It is absorbed into the body by inhalation or it can pass through clothing and be absorbed into the system through the skin.

Two of the blood gases are: hydrogen cyanide and cyanogen chloride. These act about as quickly as the nerve gases. Both blood gases are colorless, but they have a slight peach-like odor. These gases suffocate the body within fifteen minutes by locking oxygen in the blood stream preventing its transfer to the body tissues. A third blood gas is Arsine, also colorless, but with a mild garlic odor. This is a delayed action gas which destroys the kidneys and liver by robbing them of blood. It can kill within two hours or death may take as long as eleven days.

Still another group of gases are the blister agents. These are made from distilled mustard, nitrogen mustard and Lewiside. These agents are rapidly absorbed through the unprotected skin and if inhaled will fry the respiratory and digestive tracts, lung tissue and any other internal organ they may reach. These are easily recognized. Distilled mustard smells like garlic and sometimes can be seen as a palish yellow vapor; nitrogen mustard has a fishy odor, and Lewiside smells like geraniums; both are dark in concentration.

There are two other gases used in World War I that are still considered important militarily, they are: phosgene and diphosgene, often called the choking gases. Both are colorless and have the odor of new mown hay; both burn into the lungs and throat making men violently ill. Generally the victim recovers from these gases but heavy dosages can be fatal.

Bacteriological Warfare

Greenhouses are now maintained by our government to test chemicals designed to destroy plant-life. Studies are being carried out to determine the most effective way to spread plant diseases that attack wheat, barley, oats, rye, rice and cotton. Infected insects are kept constantly available at Fort Detrick, Maryland. We cultivate fleas infected with plague; ticks that carry tularemia, relapsing fever and Colorado fever; house flies riven with cholera, anthrax and dysentery; mosquitoes that carry yellow fever, malaria, and dengue fever are held at the ready. This is the backbone of our preparedness program for bacteriological warfare. Bacteria can infect men with anthrax, bacillary dysentery, undulant fever, cholera, rabies, diphtheria, tularemia, bubonic or pneumonic plague, typhoid fever, tuberculosis or other dread diseases. There is the bacteria-like micro-organism, the rickettsiae, which are usually carried by lice and ticks and which can induce various kinds of typhus and Rocky Mountain spotted fever. There are the virus carrying agents which can cause different types of encephalitis, smallpox, yellow fever, dengue fever and hepatitis. These agents can be ground into fine cloud-like mist, powder or dust and sprayed into available winds, or they can be carried in rockets, shells or bombs and introduced into water, food and drug supplies. One bomber can carry enough biological agents to infect a 34,000 square mile land area with only 450 pounds of biological agents.

Major General Chisholm, the first Director-General of the World Health Organization, speaking at a press conference in the United Nations, observed that "most of the world's inhabitants will be wiped out in any future war in which virulent bacteria now developed are used as weapons. . . . Bacteriological weapons, developed late in the Second World War, could wipe out all human life in a given area within six hours and yet leave the area inhabitable afterwards."[1]

It is reliably reported that the latest chemical and biological warfare agents carried in a single bomb could kill more people than an H-bomb. While the research being done in this area is extremely secret, an occasional suggestion of the magnitude of new discoveries appears. One example: Dr. William H. Summerson of the U. S. Army Chemical Corps reported that nerve gases are the most lethal agents that could be used in chemical warfare. These agents, he reveals, kill in minutes by overstimulating the nervous system. Some chemical agents already developed are so powerful that an aspirin-size amount of one chemical has killed 350 animals in experimentation. New gases generally have no detectable odor or color, the victim simply inhales the gas and dies before anything can be done to save him.

To the military mind these chemical and biological agents have an "advantage" over conventional and atomic

1. Montreal *Gazette*, October 14, 1949.

weapons in that target areas are not destroyed. This ob-
viates the necessity of rebuilding occupied territory.

Compunctions against killing by devious means having
considerably lessened with the advent of atomic weaponry,
it can be expected that more lethal rather than non-lethal
gases will be used in the pre-nuclear phase of future wars
involving the total commitment of the major powers.

Nuclear Deterrence

The major powers base their security on their ability
either singly or in co-operation with allies to visit upon an
aggressor massive nuclear destruction. The theory is that
faced with such certain retaliatory devastation a potential
aggressor will be deterred.

Essential to a policy of nuclear deterrence is the threat
to use nuclear weapons. The major powers have stated and
reiterated their respective threats on numerous occasions.
The United States has even taken the position that it
would be the first to use nuclear force under certain conditions.[2]

The danger to humanity lies in the fact that as the
threats to use nuclear weapons become more freely and
loosely made by an increasing number of nations, these
threats will at some point be challenged. Leaders faced
with a challenge may well elect to use small "tactical"
nuclear weapons rather than run the risk of having their
entire security position considered a bluff, for once a back-
down occurs, the enemy state will become intrigued with
the question of what other concessions can be gained by
continuing to call the bluff of their adversary. It then
becomes a game of dare, with the fate of nations and even
the fate of humanity hanging in the balance. At some

2. See: White House release as reported by the Associated Press,
March 27, 1962.

point the conceding nation may well feel that further concessions cannot be made without labeling as fraudulant its threats to use nuclear force. At this point humanity will face its darkest hour.

Our nation's policy of nuclear deterrence has not deterred the takeover of nations by subversion from within and without, nor has it prevented the domination of smaller nations by various of the major powers. It has not brought food to the hungry, freedom to the oppressed, medical attention to the ill, the halt and the lame. Our nation's policy of nuclear deterrence, to which we devote so much of our substance as a nation, has failed completely to serve us well politically, physically or morally. It does serve to prevent our fullest exploration of alternative plans for security because we are so committed to the policy politically, so wedded to it economically and so engrossed in keeping our arsenal of weapons sufficiently sophisticated to impress our opponents.

Under the policy of nuclear deterrence, if one side launches a nuclear attack it will immediately suffer annihilation in retaliation. Is this a policy of security or suicide?

The psychological effects of our commitment to this policy is revealed by a leading psychoanalyst who has written that the effect on our citizens of the constant threat of destruction is to create within them "fright, hostility, callousness, a hardening of the heart and a resulting indifference to all the values we cherish."[3] He further observes that, "Such conditions will transform us into barbarians."[4]

3. Erich Fromm, *May Man Prevail?* Doubleday-Anchor, New York, 1961.
4. *Ibid.*

In a research analysis, it has been estimated that the United States and its NATO allies would be willing to risk the possibility of having one to two hundred million people killed from the immediate effects of an initial nuclear strike. This does not include deaths from long range effects that would occur over a long period of years. It does not include two hundred million people receiving non-fatal permanent physical defects nor the 1 per cent of our children who would be deformed.[5]

One of the positive effects of our commitment to a nuclear deterrence policy is to impel our people underground as we fall victim to our own policy. A mole-like existence under the earth is hardly befitting a people once dedicated to human liberty under law and government. Yet, our present policy for the survival of our nation is steadily directing our attention toward the bowels of the earth as we prepare underground facilities in which to exist, at least for a time, when nuclear war erupts.

Nuclear deterrence is clearly a misnomer in the field of military weaponry. Rather than deter, it makes for heated competition among nations to develop new and more sophisticated and demonic devices of warfare. A military-related scientific breakthrough on one side has the effect of stimulating military research in the enemy nation. Such a breakthrough becomes not a deterrent but an incentive to other nations to increase their war potential. A significant military breakthrough could conceivably so disturb the balance of power in a critical time as to cause the doctrine of pre-emptive (preventive) war to be brought into play in a desperate effort by the weaker nation or alliance to prevent an anticipated take-over by the nation achieving the breakthrough. Actually, never in history have nations

5. Herman Kahn, *On Thermonuclear War*. Princeton Press, 1961, p. 149.

been so powerful nor had less security. We live under the threat of annihilation and we are no less blameworthy than our adversaries for the creation and continuation of the shortsighted and highly dangerous policy of nuclear deterrence. We as a nation must seek an alternative with at least the same emotional, physical and economic vigor with which we support and nurture our war machine.

Walter Lippman said in February of 1950 that, "There is no way the American people can divest themselves of the duty to search for a decent and honorable alternative to a war of extermination. They cannot sit down, fold their hands across their stomachs, saying that their search has ended, that they have reached the limits of their wisdom, that there is nothing more they can do except to make more and bigger bombs. The day we did that would mark the death of the American spirit."

We suffer from the fallacy that we have strength through arms, but five thousand years of man's recorded history should teach us that the arms race to which we are now dedicated as a nation will end in war.

We base the continued existence of our free society on our ability to act more atrociously than any conqueror in all of history. It is difficult to absorb this doctrine with equanimity; it is almost unbelievable that a nation that once stood for the ennoblement of man could now be so preoccupied with the creation of means to kill human beings by the millions. Have we lost our faith in law and government as the best means of securing the blessings of liberty and justice?

Security based primarily on armed might instead of law and government causes military power to become an all-absorbing concern, an end in itself, a substitute for a clear national goal. We may have even come to the position as a nation that thermonuclear war is a tolerable con-

cept as we burrow underground and academically calculate
the deaths of millions of peoples by means of graphs,
charts, military analyses, rationalizations, pseudo patri-
otic pronouncements, and prate barbarisms dressed in
sophisticated and scientific jargon. Surely a sickness is on
the land as we accommodate ourselves to this gross ob-
scenity.

A neo-cannibalism and self-destructive psychosis has
taken hold of us. In our state of national delusion mixed
with fear concerning the effectiveness of nuclear deterrence
as a policy, we have lost sight of the motivating value on
which our republic was founded, i.e., the supreme worth of
the individual human life. Lester Pearson phrased it well
when he said "we prepare for war like giants as we seek
peace like pigmies."[6]

6. See: Nobel Prize Address of Lester Pearson, *New York Times*,
November 17, 1957.

"I may indicate briefly what to me constitutes the essence of the crisis of our time. It concerns the relationship of the individual to society. The individual has become more conscious than ever of his dependence upon society. But he does not experience this dependence as a positive asset, as an organic tie, as a protective force, but rather as a threat to his natural rights, or even to his economic existence. Moreover, his position in society is such that the egotistical drives of his make-up are constantly being accentuated, while his social drives, which are by nature weaker, progressively deteriorate. All human beings, whatever their position in society, are suffering from this process of deterioration. Unknowingly prisoners of their own egotism, they feel insecure, lonely, and deprived of the naive, simple and unsophisticated enjoyment of life. Man can find meaning in life, short and perilous as it is, only through devoting himself to society."

—ALBERT EINSTEIN

THE ECONOMICS OF WAR

Unquestionably, if we turn all of the productive power of the United States to the production of useful consumer goods and services, our standard of living would be markedly higher than it now is. Economic prosperity, rather than depending on armament production and repeated world crisis, depends on the services available and the flow of useful consumer goods to our citizens. Spending by the government alone does not keep our industries prosperous; it is rather the combination of economic activity by individual citizens, businesses and governmental agencies that causes our economy to expand healthfully. Thus, if the government spends less, taxes levied on the individual citizen could be lowered which would in turn cause the consuming public to have more money with which to purchase goods and services.

It was in 1946 and 1947 that the United States witnessed its largest cutback in military spending since World War II, yet business and employment remained good. This was of course in part due to the large backlog of savings in the hands of consumers, but economists are well aware that a cut in federal taxation creates new purchasing power and that man's thirst for new things is virtually unquenchable.

There is the great need for new programs in economic education. It has been estimated by J. T. Bodet, former Director General of UNESCO, that one billion two hundred million men and women live in an invisible inner dungeon, i.e., they cannot read. Adequate programs to provide decent housing have not been possible here and abroad due to the magnitude and drain on the world economy of military spending. In 1958, for example, the United States had seven and one-half million people employed in war-related work (including members of the armed forces) while spending forty-five billion dollars for "defense."

If world armament spending could be reduced to, say, five billion, that necessary to support an effective United Nations police detachment, then over a ten-year period some 200 to 500 billion dollars that would otherwise go into armaments in the United States would be available for tax savings and non-war-related governmental expenditures. Literally billions of dollars would be saved in taxes and still other billions spent for the following projects, among others:

1. Aid to world development.
2. Public health, hospitals, medical care and research.
3. National resources conservation projects such as waterways, recreation areas, and reforestation, desalination of sea water.
4. Old age and child welfare and other social security needs.
5. Adequate school buildings and teacher salaries.
6. An increase in the number of research grants in non-military projects.
7. Slum clearance and urban renewal.
8. Greatly expanded educational programs for the entire country.

Hunger is at the base of much of the world's misery. Still, great areas of potentially productive land lie unused for lack of sufficient amounts of fresh water. The great desert areas of the United States, the 4.5 million square miles of Arab desert (the Sahara alone is as big as the United States), the Gobi desert and other such unproductive areas can be used to supply food for the hungry masses of the world. Desalination of ocean water can make these areas bloom and together with present agricultural land underproducing or intentionally abandoned in the United States and elsewhere they can insure that the world's population can be well fed in the future. Dual desalination and electric energy plants run by nuclear power can supply adequate fresh water and energy for all mankind for thousands of years to come.

Clearly man's present rate of populating the world must be decreased. But we can limit our population without liquidating it. Planned parenthood through universal education in methods of effective contraception, not nuclear bombs, must be the reducing force in the population explosion. Parochial governmental action will not suffice to meet this vital problem. It requires a universal approach that must be co-ordinated by a world authority.

Minimal estimates place the need for new classrooms at 130,000 and we need 230,000 new teachers in the United States. We are now confronted with the fact that almost as many teachers are leaving the profession as are entering it; this in the face of a rapidly increasing population. Also some 46,000 teachers receive less than $2,500 a year.

Some 325,000 lives are lost each year through inadequate medical care, and 1,200,000 hospital beds are needed to care for those in need of hospitalization in the U.S. alone. A large number of these beds are needed in mental and chronic-disease hospitals and nursing homes. It has been estimated that 2.5 million people reside in areas with no acceptable general hospital beds, another 25,000 people live where there are less than two acceptable hospital beds per 1,000 people.

There is no question but that our nation needs more public health clinics; more medical schools; more people in medical research to wipe out such enemies of mankind as mental illness, heart disease and cancer.

We need better roads and communications, flood control and other conservation projects. The military departments of the government now hold over 31.3 million acres of land in the continental United States that could be used for public recreation, housing for our expanding population, water power projects, mineral supply and wildlife conservation.

One of the tragedies of our time is the fact that we store our surplus food in warehouses while millions over the world go hungry. Actually, there is no food surplus when viewed from an international perspective; the problem lies in getting the food into the hands of the needy. This problem will be solved under the pressure of the increasing world population; and when it is, lands not now under cultivation will be needed to produce food for the world. The tillable soil now out of production in the United States because of "surpluses" and military establishments can be utilized to supply food for the hungry people of the world. What a shame that in a nation of free enterprise and great production potential our citizens are paid not to produce food when millions of people over the world are hungry. The freedom of the farmer to pursue his calling has been lost to the system of anarchy among nations. Clearly, our nation has proven it is unable unilaterally or by regional agreement to bring the American farmers' produce to the peoples of the world.

Research grant monies now used for essentially military related projects could be diverted to programs of world development. The savings that could be effected by reduced government military spending, in addition to providing tax relief for all Americans, would allow the government to turn its attention to the need for schools, housing, hospitals, parks and roads. This would not have to be done by the federal government; state taxes could be raised a modest amount and these needs could thus be supplied by the states themselves. The federal government's role in the economy of our nation could be greatly reduced. Such increase in state taxation would in no way equal, but be far less than, the savings to the individual and to the corporate taxpayer which would result from the reduced spending by the federal government.

Not only our own citizens, but people throughout the world, hunger for many things other than food. Supplying these needs would be far easier in an atmosphere of relaxed world tension when old inhibitions raised in the name of national security could be lowered safely as an effective world authority filled the power vacuum and provided the security between nations now so desperately but ineffectively sought by unilateral means.

There is no doubt that there would of necessity be a shift in employment if military expenditures were cut. For example, 100 per cent of the orders of some plants in California, Washington, Kansas and Texas are based on military contracts. It would be largely the function of the government to assist the employees of these—and other plants in a similar situation—in their transition to develop new skills or to assist them in finding jobs in which they could utilize their old skills in non-military type work.

Certainly the government should help to give these people a fervor for making their job changes, emphasizing that such change would be in the national interest and the worker's personal contribution to national security and world peace. It must be made clear that a change from high government spending is necessary to the future of America. The occupational shifts that would result from a peace economy must be related to the individual interests of those affected by our shift in economic emphasis. Obviously, military spending cutbacks would be planned and announced well in advance.

Most of the materials used in military production have peacetime uses. For example, metal that goes into bombers could go into buildings; civilian aircraft production can replace, in part, war plane production. Activity in the missile field could be switched to the space program. In the electronics field materials that go into ballistic missiles could be used in hospitals and schools.

In such an economy, we could serve mankind by serving the world. To further stimulate demand, we should lend money to the other nations with the stipulation that the money loaned be spent in the United States for products manufactured here.

In those areas where employees were hardest hit, the government would make provision for the requisite education and relocation. Temporary financial support could be made available if requested by the individual citizen or firm. Government retraining schools, employment and placement services to assist in re-education and relocation would undoubtedly be needed.

At present there is no question but that our taxes are used to pay large sums to industrialists to produce weapons of war, and to our farmers not to produce food. This irony certainly does not reflect the true greatness of America.

When military appropriation bills come before Congress, it is quite natural for owners of plants producing for the Pentagon to make it known that it would be wise for their employees to ask their senators and representatives in Washington to fight military cutbacks. Farmers tend to favor continual price supports for agricultural products and the inertia thus generated perpetuates the status quo in both heavy industry and agriculture.

It is clear that severance pay and opportunities for education and vocational training will be essential in the transition period from a war to a peace economy. Bonuses and loans for housing and businesses together with increased educational opportunities would also be supplied in connection with a peace transition program and would be much preferable to the spending that is now required to maintain the present war system economics of the nation.

The billion dollar poverty eradication program placed into effect by President Johnson in the United States is but an indication of what could be done both in this country and throughout the world if the war system is replaced by enforceable world law.

The Area Redevelopment Act, together with more recent legislation in the field of poverty eradication, provides for the training and retraining of unemployed persons who are paid at the state unemployment compensation level while retraining. Similar legislation of an expanded nature could well be used in the transition of this nation to a peaceful economy. Obviously, such legislation would have to cover the training and retraining of those already employed who wished to learn a non-military-related skill or who were seeking to adapt their armament production skill to another type of employment. This is the type of legislation that could be used to supply the needs of workers affected by cutbacks in military spending to assist them in their efforts to return to peace-related employment. Just a slight reduction in government arms expenditure would release large sums for retraining and rehabilitation. For example, a 10 per cent reduction in military spending by our government for one year would pay for our present vocational training program for the next 250 years.[1]

Governmental agencies of the Reconstruction Finance Corporation, the Federal Housing Administration, The Office of Defense Mobilization type could provide guidance and assistance to effect mobilization for peace. A new supervisory agency to co-ordinate the activities of the transition to a peaceful economy should be created at the federal, state and local levels. Tax credits and benefits to encourage prompt business readjustment would be provided.

The Small Business Administration would assist with financial backing for small business firms adversely affected. Tax carryover provisions to encourage plants to hold their workers during the change-over period should be supplied. The possibility of a reduction of the national debt over the long run through reduced government spending would be a concomitant to a move away from military spending, although emphasis should be placed on the fact that this would be a long-range, not an immediate result.

The successful and efficient change from high military spending should be of the highest import to our people and our government. Full participation should be encouraged by every citizen. The philosophy of working as a nation for a better America that stands for peace, liberty and the betterment of mankind should be emphasized.

1. See address of Adlai E. Stevenson, *American Bar Association Journal*, Vol. 50, pp. 921-924.

Discussions in labor unions, chambers of commerce, churches, civic organizations must be encouraged. There must be planning at every level coupled with intensive research.

If we are to present to the world a peaceful image; if we are to be an example of an enlightened democratic political structure; if we are to show the world that we can prosper without a military economy; if we are to show the world that we believe in peace, law and world co-operation for constructive purposes; if we are to demonstrate that we can apply our great powers of production to meet the needs of man; if we are to demonstrate the basic morality of the democratic free-enterprise system, we must begin the process of getting out of the war business. We must change our principal governmental emphasis from military to peaceful activity.

Literally billions of dollars are paid out each year in military and civilian payrolls by our armed services. Millions go into construction, food, services, supplies and housing. Millions of taxpayer dollars get into the hands of servicemen and civilian employees of the military and then into the cash registers of local merchants, landlords, and banking institutions. As servicemen retire additional millions are passed to them in their civilian status; these dollars then flow into the national economy.

To the local merchants, the servicemen are good customers who buy new and used automobiles, boating and other sporting goods, spend their money on luxuries, in restaurants and clothing stores. The families of servicemen help to spend the taxpayer's money. In short, every merchant in a military area is likely to receive more dollars because of the presence of the military and would therefore oppose any threat to the status quo.

Military Waste

Waste in spending military dollars is not unknown. The Air Force closed a base in Racine, Wisconsin after spending $15,000,000 of the proposed $80,000,000.

Senator Paul Douglas, on April 28, 1959, said that the Defense Department had sold six billion dollars worth of surplus property for two hundred million dollars, and Representative Edward F. Herbert of Louisiana, on June 3, 1959, said the Air Force had been overcharged thirty million dollars on fourteen contracts. It is interesting to note that 80-90 per cent of all defense contracts are let without competitive bidding.

Tremendous sums of money have been applied toward the creation of weapons that never panned out. For example, the Skybolt missile program was canceled by the Pentagon after the government had spent 353 million dollars for research on this project. The atomic airplane program was shelved after one billion dollars had been expended over a ten-year period. The jet seaplane P6M Seamaster was washed out after 387 million dollars had been spent. The boron exotic fuel development program and plant construction work were canceled after 240 million dollars were spent. The Army's heavy M-103, 62-ton tank program was dropped after several hundred million dollars had been spent towards its development; only a few dozen were ever actually built. The Regulus 11 designed to be fired from surfaced submarines was dropped after 146 million dollars had been spent. The Navaho missile, a long range ramjet with a self-contained guidance system, was dropped after an expenditure of 680 million dollars.

The world's first atomic power aircraft carrier was launched at a cost of four hundred and thirty-five million dollars. At the same time a new hospital was opened in Elizabeth City, North Carolina, at a cost of three million dollars. Thus some one hundred and forty-five completely equipped county hospitals could have been built for the cost of this nuclear carrier. If it were not for the arms race, new hospitals would not only be possible in the United States, but in all parts of the world.

Sylvia Porter, noted economic columnist, has stated, "While sanity cries out that we should greet with delight a chance for relief from the forty-one billion dollars a year of our money the Pentagon is spending, the fact is that every time there has been a suggestion for major cut in arms spending, the stock market has done a tailspin."

Miss Porter in another article entitled "Nikita May End Recession," which dealt in part with Khrushchev's reaction to our U-2 spy flights over Russia, said, "It could be that the debacle at Paris will just about eliminate the danger of an important recession in 1960 or 1961."

Extensive planning must precede and accompany the transition to a peace-oriented economy, as tremendous sums of money now being spent by the government for war material would be diverted to other uses. In this connection, some figures relative to the unit costs of armament are interesting:

1 fighter plane—$1,000,000+
1 bomber—$8,000,000 to $20,000,000
1 ICBM missile—$2,000,000 to $13,000,000
1 nuclear submarine—$85,000,000 to $105,000,000
1 destroyer—$27,000,000+
1 280 millimeter atomic cannon—$800,000+
1 anti-missile missile—$20,000+

One of the chief causes of recessions is that purchasing power does not keep up with production of goods, thus wages must be kept high as production of consumer goods increases in the future peace economy. People must be kept employed in the period of shift from military spending. Tax savings and federal assistance can increase purchasing power and demand for consumer goods and services during the transition period. Employment would be kept high by programs of retraining and public works including the building of schools, hospitals, housing, roads, flood control projects, irrigation projects, urban renewal and conservation programs of the CCC type. We could get our farmers back into production again as the sale of surplus farm commodities in a world of reduced tensions would present no insuperable problems. It would be in this atmosphere that the genius of our scientists and the sweat of our laborers and the hopes of our children would not be subverted by a continuation of our preoccupation with the business of war. The savings effected by a shift away from military emphasis would enable us to have a more adequate social security program. Private pension plans by industry would become more widespread in a peace economy. But there is great need for the government to address itself to the problems attendant to a shift to non-military production.

Do We Have a Vested Interest In War?

Of great interest and concern is the fact that the federal government spends five million dollars of the taxpayers money each hour chiefly for military related projects. Do Americans have a vested interest in war? Secretary of Defense, Charles W. Wilson, speaking before a House subcommittee on January 20, 1957, said, "I have said to a number of my friends that one of the serious things about this defense business is that so many Americans are getting a vested interest in it; properties, business, jobs, employment, votes, opportunities for promotion and advancement, bigger salaries for scientists, and all that. It is troublesome business."

In 1960, the military budget alone of the United States represented four hundred times our contribution to the United Nations. Each year the average United States citizen contributes an amount to our military budget equal to more than twice the per capita annual income of his counterpart in the underdeveloped world.

About 9 to 10 per cent of the United States labor force depends upon defense expenditures for its livelihood.

Some 84 per cent of the federal research expenditures go for national security purposes.

Military agencies hold properties valued at one hundred and seventy billion dollars.

The Defense Department controls 31.3 million acres of land.

The Defense Department owns 3,553 military installations in the United States alone.

Veterans, their dependents, and survivors constitute 45 per cent of the United States population and as of June 30, 1959, more than 99 billion dollars had been spent on veterans programs.

If the costs of veterans' benefits and interest on the national debt are added to the expenditures for the United States military programs and defense-related activities at home and abroad the combined costs would represent 79.9 per cent of the national budget.

Of the present national debt, over 270.4 billion dollars was accumulated during war years, i.e., during the years of 1917-19, 1939-46, and 1950-54.

The United States' expenditures for annual defense programs average more than $250 per citizen per year whereas our contribution as a nation to all United Nations programs comes to less than 65 cents per citizen each year.

The burden of armament that restricts our production and international trade holds back underdeveloped areas which presently have a pitiable per capita income. The people of India and Pakistan have an average yearly income of $60 to $70 per year; this is below the average for the underdeveloped world which is about $100. It is estimated that the world spends well over 100 billion dollars each year in the arms race. These dollars are virtually stolen from the needy people of the underdeveloped world. A system of world security under law could well mean to mankind a trillion-dollar saving in armament spending over a ten-year period when viewed in the light of present rising costs and armament outlays by the nations of the earth.

This current financial burden on all men does mean full-time employment in the armed forces for 3 to 4 million men and women plus an additional 3 to 4 million civilians who engage directly in the manufacture of armaments. This constitutes a great impediment to any disarmament efforts.

In the Soviet Union the proportion of the national product devoted to military purposes is even higher than in the United States. It would certainly seem logical that as a matter of self-interest the Soviets would be eager to relieve their economy of this financial burden and to turn their attention to the production of consumer goods and services which they so greatly desire and need.

The numerical strength of the combined armed forces of the United States exceeds 2,489,000 men and women. The number of civilian employees of the Defense Department and other defense agencies is in excess of 1,062,300, making a total number of persons engaged in military ac-

tivities for the United States at 3,551,300, not counting
those millions of persons employed in military-related industries. This latter number is estimated to be between 3.5
and 4 million. Thus, out of a total labor force of 72
million persons in the United States, 6.5 to 7.5 million
derive their income directly from military expenditures.
These figures do not count the 177,800 foreign nationals
working in our overseas bases, nor does it include the 1,-
082,700 military reservists who receive regular pay from
the military budget. In addition there are employees of
the Veterans Administration, Soldiers Home, American
Battle Monuments Commission; the total number of
these employees is 173,800.

In 1960, Robert E. Bower, Director of the Bureau of
Social Science Research, said, "We can safely predict that
starting this year there will be a marked increase in the
numbers retiring from military service until, within a few
years, we will have over a million retired officers and
men." The average age of these former military people
will be in the low forties and their military retirement
pay in the aggregate will come to more than one billion
dollars per year by 1964.

There are 325,400 students in the Army, Navy, Air
Force ROTC units together with 2,243 Marine officer
candidates. These ROTC programs are given in 233
colleges and 289 high schools. The Army and Navy
auxiliaries are conducting training at 53 colleges while
the Air Force is training additional students at 175 colleges.

Defense spending has acted as a life saver for many
plants during times of economic recession and as economic
salvation for many individuals in times of unemployment.

The government buys 80 per cent of all the aircraft,
missiles and space vehicles manufactured in the United

States. For example, the Boeing Aircraft Company is dependent upon the government for 99.6 per cent of its sales. Work on missiles accounts for 25 per cent of the total manufacturing employment in the San Diego and San Jose, California areas, and more than 12 per cent of the total work force in metropolitan Los Angeles.

In addition to military contracts, the military installations in the United States account for a government expenditure of 11 billion dollars a year. This payroll is equal to one and one-half times the combined payrolls of the iron and steel industries and more than twice that of the automobile industry. In Texas the military payroll is equal to 40 per cent of the wages and salaries paid by all manufacturers. People, industries and localities react violently when defense contracts are cut back and military installations close. Senator Javits, referring in the Senate to the rapid upswing in defense awards in the state of California, noted that his own state of New York contributed more to the federal budget than California, but was getting fewer defense contracts. Senator Butler of Maryland told the Senate that, "I intend to press for a full and complete investigation of this policy of California first and foremost until I am completely satisfied that performance, and not influence from former generals and admirals on the boards of California companies, is responsible for the consistent winning of contracts by these goldenplated state firms."

Military Influence on Government Spending

It was in 1959 that a special House subcommittee was commissioned to investigate the employment of retired military personnel by defense contractors. The work by this committee revealed that 261 generals and admirals

and 485 retired officers above the rank of colonel and
Navy captain were then employed by the companies that
manufacture 88 per cent of our military weapons. For
example, the General Dynamics Corporation had five
brigadier generals and nineteen rear admirals working for
it; the chairman of its board of directors, Frank Pace, a
former Secretary of the Army, with General Joseph Mc-
Nerney, a member of its Board of Directors. North American Aviation Company employs one general and six rear
admirals. General Electric employs three major generals
and five rear admirals. Lockheed Aircraft Corporation
employs five brigadier generals and nineteen rear admirals.

Ohio Representative Charles A. Vanik, speaking in the
House, referred to "the strange paradox that bad news
for the world should be good news for the stock market."
Continuing he said, "The defense group of stocks, air-
crafts, missiles, and electronics, as well as steels took a
sharp rise in the trading which was the heaviest in more
than a year after the collapse of the Summit Conference"
(between Eisenhower and Khrushchev).

This frantic spending by the federal government for
armaments has unquestionably been not only at the ex-
pense of the taxpayers but has taken monies away from
vital peacetime programs. According to Seymour Harris,
Professor of Political Economy at Harvard, "The government has been underspending for years, under the pressure of cold war costs and budgetary stress in such vital
areas as education, urban renewal, housing, power, polu-
tion, irrigation, conservation, flood control, navigation,
forestation, airport improvement, highways, hospitals,
health services and social security."

Again, in this great spending there is great waste—
86.7 per cent of defense contracts are awarded without
competitive bidding. Senator Paul H. Douglas of Illinois

has estimated that the waste is between two and three billion dollars a year because of lack of competitive bidding. To support this contention he showed the Senate ten items bought under contract which cost the government many times the market price. Such items as a small wrench set for which the Army paid $29.00 could be purchased by an average citizen at a local store for $3.89. He showed the Senate a $.25 lamp socket which was sold to the Navy for $2.10. Representative Frank Kowalski of Connecticut has assailed the Defense Department for using 20,000 enlistees as chauffeurs, laundry boys, and maid servants. It was his estimate that the armed forces could save the taxpayer 250 million dollars a year by stopping such practices.

The Defense Department is our nation's biggest business, owning 278,237 buildings and 3,553 military installations in the United States exclusive of Alaska and the United States territories. In addition, the Department of Defense leases other facilities at home and abroad and occupies 250 major bases in thirty-six foreign countries. It is interesting to note that the Defense Department's holdings are larger than the combined areas of the states of New Hampshire, Vermont, Massachusetts, Rhode Island, New Jersey, Delaware and Maryland.[2]

The military business is a boon to many areas. In Utah already new missile plants have added 63 million dollars to the wallets of the workers of that state. And one out of every two Utahans is employed at a weapons plant. The Sperry Utah Engineering Laboratory, a division of Sperry Rand Corporation, has the second biggest payroll in the Salt Lake City area and its chief manufacturing contract is to produce the Army's Sergeant missile

2. *The Big Hand in Your Pocket* published by the American Friends Service Committee, Philadelphia, Pennsylvania, October, 1960.

system. Also in the Salt Lake City area the Bacchus works of the Hercules Powder Company contracted to build the third stage of the Air Force Minute Man intercontinental ballistic missile as well as the second stage of the Navy's Polaris missile. One fourth of all personal income of the citizens of Utah is derived from government sources. The largest employer in the state of Utah is the Hill Air Force Base, which has 12,000 civilians on its payroll. These civilians are engaged in the assembly of Minute Man missiles. Joseph Rosenblatt, a Salt Lake City industrialist, said, "It is no use standing up in Rotary and talking about the evils of government spending and then, after lunch, going back to the business which is dependent upon it." Congressman David King said, "In Washington I argued to beat the band to get more defense dollars, yet at the same time, I am worried about what it is doing to our people." And Marriner Ecoles, former Chairman of the Board of Governors of the Federal Reserve System, said, "I'd like to see our prosperity based on something more solid and less destructive than the missile industry."

The report of the Committee on Foreign Relations, Subcommittee on Disarmament, entitled *Control and Reduction of Armaments*[3] is of great interest. The Senate group had this to say, "The Subcommittee is of the firm conviction that efforts to achieve the control and reduction of armaments should not be hampered in any way on the grounds of their economic consequences. The ultimate benefits of disarmament are so great that we must proceed toward this goal despite any monetary problems in the economic sphere.

"Expenditures for national security amount roughly to 2/3rd's of the Federal budget. This includes funds for the United States defense establishment, the military

3. September, 1957.

portion of the Atomic Energy Program, military aid to friendly nations, and the stock piling of scarce materials.

"About half of the research being carried on in this country is financed by the defense budget. In view of these factors, it would be foolish to conclude that any substantial reduction in armament would have no impact on the economy.

"On the other hand, the primary impetus for the prosperity and growth of this nation does not rest on defense spending.

"Dominant forces behind the growth of national income are the large scale investment programs of industry, residential and industrial construction, the high level of consumer spending, the expansion of foreign trade, and increasing expenditures of local and state governments.

"Moreover, many needs of the American people remain unfulfilled, among them more schools and hospitals, improved roads and highway systems, and adequate water resources including power. Expansion of the peacetime activities of many private industries has been held up due to defense requirements. Back accumulated demand for commercial aircraft should be noted. Peaceful uses of atomic energy must also be speeded if this country is to maintain its leadership in an increasingly competitive field internationally.

"High taxes have precluded consumers from numerous articles to enrich their lives. Large amounts of the earnings of our corporations have supplied the government with revenue through taxation and, thus, have caused postponement of new enterprise. The large defense budget has also been a factor in the current inflation.

"In the view of the Subcommittee the above factors point to the conclusion that a disarmament agreement which permitted a cutback in defense expenditures would provide this country with enormous opportunities. Not only would the citizens of this country benefit from a rechanneling of funds from defense to constructive peacetime projects, but the people of the entire world would profit and world resources could be used to ease the burdens of mankind.

"Of particular need is an inquiry into possible adjustments of individual industries which are presently channeling a large part of their production into defense requirements. In this respect private industries and private organizations might make a contribution by undertaking studies of certain key segments of the economy.

"Government agencies such as the Office of Defense Mobilization, the Federal Reserve Board, the President's Council of Economic Advisers and the Department of Defense, Treasury, Commerce and Labor are especially encouraged to devote more time to determine appropriate offices and programs to be instituted if a substantial cutback in armaments were to occur."

The report goes on to show that the problem of disarmament in the view of the committee would have two aspects: The first (which we have covered) is economic, the second is legal. "If the United States is to continue to lead in the search for world peace; if we are to diminish the threat of the terrible third world war which hangs so heavily upon us and which requires us to sacrifice so much in the way of human and material resources we need the understanding, the inspiration, and the active concern of the American in all walks of life. The search for peace, freedom, and justice for all mankind must go on."[4]

Government expenditures represent 20 per cent of all expenditures. The quantity of goods the government purchases from private industry amounts to many times that

4. *Ibid.*

bought by the largest corporations. For each of the 2,500,-
000 men in the armed forces $18,000.00 is spent each
year. This amounts to about nine times the per capita
government expenditure for the nation as a whole.

A widely read national magazine said, "Wall Street
had a short but violent case of the jitters this week. A
selling wave set stock prices tumbling in the sharpest correction since the bull market resumed in the last year.
Selling was largely attributed to a 'peace scare' touched
off by the news that Khrushchev and Eisenhower were
exchanging visits."[5] Then in the nationally syndicated
column of Sylvia Porter there was the statement that "no
matter how much the experts emphasized the rallies and
talk about overdue correction, the fact is that the breaks
were triggered by fear that talks [between Khrushchev
and Eisenhower] might lead to lessening world tensions,
a slash in our military spending and therefore a slump
in our economy."[6]

Military spending is actually the life food of the contractors who are engaged in the production of armaments.
It is therefore no wonder that proposed reduction and
cuts in military spending are attacked and resisted with
every power at their command. There is no question but
that many of our citizens have a vested interest in our
military economy. Thus, it can be expected that the general but relatively weak and unorganized sentiment for
reduction of taxation and inflationary pressure through
reduction in military spending will be resisted wherever
this general sentiment seeks to take concrete form.

Dr. R. S. Winslow, Professor of Economics and Director of the Bureau of Business Service and Research
School for the University of North Carolina's School of

5. Taken from *Business Week*, August 15, 1959.
6. Sylvia Porter, August 19, 1959.

Business Administration, has said, "The suggestion that reduction in military expenditures can be offset by tax reductions and a step-up in expenditures for needed public services may be a good one; certainly it sounds more like common sense than madness." But he goes on to point out that the beating of plow shares into pruning hooks is becoming increasingly difficult.[7]

Government Grants

There is now the very real question of whether or not educational institutions in their scientific research can maintain their objective standards and vitality in the face of tremendous government subsidies for military research offered the staffs of institutions of higher learning. Dr. Philip H. Abelson, editor of *Science*, the magazine of the American Association for the Advancement of Science, has expressed the concern that science is being used increasingly as a front for technological leaf-raking; a new and sophisticated word for Public Work Administration-type pump priming. The average man, not understanding the technologies of modern science, numbly goes along with monumental expenditures for military research and in bewilderment sees billions of dollars appropriated for a multitude of military projects. Research grants and related projects may well be wooing our most able scientists away from their main task of basic research and undermining their integrity as scholars. Universities are attracted by the possibility of acquiring new and expensive equipment while scholars themselves are attracted by the

7. Source: an article by R. S. Winslow entitled, "Can We Afford to Declare Peace?" in the October 18, 1959 issue of the Raleigh *News and Observer*.

large sums of money made available to them to pursue
their first love—research. But it is the federal government, not the scientists or the universities, that delineates
the areas of emphasis; therein lies the danger to our country and to all mankind. This danger is well illustrated by
the federally directed emphasis of scientists within the
last twenty-five years. In the absence of an equal emphasis
on research in the humanities, our research has become
dangerously controlled and out of balance.

It is essential that research activities and development
funds be used primarily for the development of basic research and secondly to applied research. The government
emphasis is on the development of highly specialized and
immediately utilitarian knowledge. The National Science
Foundation is exceptional in that 100 per cent of its research grants to universities is directed toward basic research. However, the National Aeronautics and Space
Administration earmarks only 30 per cent of their grants
for basic research; the Atomic Energy Commission directs
77 per cent of its research budget to development work
and the Department of Defense applies 86 per cent of
its budget to development work and only 14 per cent to
basic research. Thus, there is increasing danger that
federal blandishments will create a breed of kept scientists whose activities are directed by the federal government toward utilitarian ends that are war related, leaving
basic research, the very foundation of long run non-military progress, in a strictly low-budget category. Continuation and expansion of this present federal interposi-
tion—particularly in the scientific fields—will do great
damage to our educational system and to our nation.

Taxes

Congress was empowered by the Sixteenth Amendment to levy an individual income tax in 1913 when a sufficient number of states—36 at that time—had ratified the proposed amendment.

This proposal had its roots deep in American history. In 1643 Massachusetts levied a faculty tax, the theory being that every man should contribute to the needs of society according to his ability. In 1862 the federal government adopted an income tax to help finance the Civil War and the Supreme Court declared this tax to be constitutional. It was abandoned in 1872. It was enacted again in 1894, but was ruled unconstitutional by the Supreme Court in 1895. An amendment to the Constitution, put through in 1913, authorized the Congress "to lay and collect taxes on income . . . ." Thereby our present federal income tax was established.

Virginia state senator Richard E. Byrd, father of United States Senator Harry F. Byrd, fearing the income tax said, "A hand from Washington would be stretched out and placed upon every man's business; the eye of the Federal inspector will be in every man's countinghouse."

In the first year of the federal income tax a married taxpayer with two dependents and an annual income of ten thousand dollars was taxed sixty dollars by the federal government. Today his tax would be over twenty times that amount.

The United States has the most severe income tax in all the world. This unreasonable extraction is characteristic of despotism, not freedom. The war of independence was fought ostensibly to keep "swarms of officers from harassing our people" and "government [from] eating into their substance." Our present income tax, used sub-stantially for the feeding of our war machines, constitutes a perversion of our democratic ideals and sends people on a mad scurry to find loopholes in the tax law and devise means to limit their tax liabilities even to the extent of curbing their initiative and production.

It is interesting to note how today's high income tax rates began to be imposed on the American people. Rates in excess of 50 per cent were invoked during World War I and continued up to 1922. Rates were cut to a maximum of 25 per cent in 1925. Rates again rose in the depression and in World War II. Maximum rates were 63 per cent in 1932; 79 per cent in 1936; 88 per cent in 1942 and 94 per cent in 1944. The fact is that we have never gotten very far from the extreme rate progression invoked during World War II.

The emergency character of our excessive income tax has not abated since World War II, but has become an appendage to our way of life in spite of minimal rate re-ductions to stimulate the economy. The present income tax strikes at the vitals of our nation's economic strength, aside from the gross immorality of its basic purpose: to sup-port the most diabolical war machine the world has ever seen. Individual effort and enterprise is being daily curbed by the confiscatory nature of our income tax. What has happened to the individual property rights of our people and to our "free" society when such large percent-ages of individual incomes are taken by the government? Have we not here lost a measure of our freedom to the international system of anarchy? Are we not paying an enormous economic price and debasing ourselves morally for an ungoverned world of supposedly sovereign nations? Are not the baying jackals of the Internal Revenue Service increasingly making inroads into our time, our efforts and our freedoms? Does not the present income tax, 70 per cent—80 per cent of which goes for war purposes, degenerate our moral stature, stultify individual effort and unconscionably encumber our system of free enterprise? It is truly but another manifestation of our present commitment to the war system.

"The dilemma of our age, with its infinite possibilities of self-destruction, is how to grow out of the world of armaments into a world of international security, based on law."

—DAG HAMMARSKJOLD

NATIONAL SOVEREIGNTY
AND HUMAN NEED

Today's Christian is bound to wonder if he is not rendering everything to Caesar and very little to God. Are we neglecting our duty to work for the love of God, to heal bodies, not mutilate and destroy them? Are we feeding the hungry not creating hunger by our military emphasis? Are we casting out demons of fear and hate rather than nurturing them? Are we damning men or calling them to repentance?

These are questions that must be squarely faced by the citizens of all Christian nations, particularly the citizens of the United States.

But on non-religious terms, the 75 per cent of each American tax dollar spent for war and the consequences of war is outrageous and our federal income tax confiscatory. Napoleon described war as the "business of barbarians." But for years our nation, the leading nation of the world, has been engaged in this form of barbarism, as the cold war business of making armaments has become so engrained in our society as to cause President Eisenhower to say, "In the councils of government we must guard against the acquisition of unwarranted influence, whether sought or unsought, by the military industrial complex. The prospect of domination of the nation's scholars by the Federal government, project allocations, and power of money . . . is gravely to be regarded." He went on to caution against a permanent armaments industry of vast proportions and an immense military establishment.[1] This admonition coming from a forty-year veteran of the army was surprising to many observers; particularly in view of the fact that the spokesman was the President of the United States.

Thus, it is that we may have lost control or sovereignty over our own government. This is to say, that if 75 per cent of each tax dollar that goes to Washington is spent for the materials and consequences of war, surely this could not be a moral choice or the intention of the nation's founding fathers. It would be fair to say that the high taxes now paid by our citizens are not the free choice of the great majority of American citizens. These expenditures to perpetuate this barbaric business to which this nation is now committed is the result not of our free choice, but is the result of conditions in a world in which there is not sufficient international authority to act for nations as a deterrent to aggressive war. Of far more significance is the fact that in attempting unilaterally to act as this deterrent our nation has undertaken something that it cannot sustain: an undertaking that places us in a morally untenable and economically impossible position of acting as law and policeman for the world. This is rightly the business of an international authority. Yet, we are presently engaged in the business of trying to impose ourselves as the military police of the world. This brings us as a nation neither economic nor military security. It does lead us constantly to the brink of war and bankruptcy.

1. From President Eisenhower's final radio address to the nation; January, 1961.

As a nation, we claim to champion freedom, but military conscription of our youth, which, too, has become a part of our way of life, is the antithesis of freedom and is in effect involuntary servitude. Not only do we waste the economic resources of this great nation, but the cloud of conscription hangs over the heads of its young people.

Certainly the involuntary servitude of our youth would not be the free choice of our nation's people. It is rather an obligation placed upon them by a government faced with the fact that there is among nations no arbiter that can singly and effectively act as a deterrent to international warfare.

We have then lost to the system of anarchy among nations control over our youth and our economic resources. The great paradox of our time is that many of those who claim to champion American sovereignty do all in their power to prevent the attainment of world law under which conscription could be abolished and the wasteful expenditure of our nation's wealth for war purposes stopped.

When President Truman relieved General MacArthur of his command in Korea, MacArthur had not been content with his role of repelling the aggressor in Korea, but had himself become an aggressor by extending the action beyond the 38th Parallel into Northern Korea to the very borders of China, provoking the Chinese to enter the Korean war with a result that many Americans were needlessly killed. Yet in the face of this, Columbia College created a $500,000 endowment for a "Douglas MacArthur" chair in history. The City of Norfolk has renovated its old courthouse at an expenditure of one half million dollars to house the general's remains and memorabilia, which includes 150 chests of papers, correspondence and battle plans; 123 American and foreign decorations and battle trophies; gifts from world leaders;

and, uniforms including such personal emblems as his special hat, dark glasses and corn cob pipe. Should these be the object of our reverence? Are actors in this horrendous spectacle that seeks to substitute violence for law and order the true patriots of our time? It is not a shame that the words "sovereignty" and "patriotism" have been appropriated by those who worship our ancestors but who lack their political imagination and faith in government; who live in the past rather than face the needs of the future; who equate militarism with patriotism and do all in their power to prevent the advancement of the rule of law among nations?

One of the complaints usually leveled at communism is that it substitutes in importance the state for the individual. But each time a young person of the West is conscripted against his will there is additional evidence that Western nations too, at least to this extent, deprive their citizens of freedom in the name of the state.

There is nothing basically un-American about surrendering national sovereignty for the good of the people. Quite the contrary, such limitations of national sovereignty were written into the Constitution of the United States reserving to the individual states and depriving the federal government of certain powers by means of the Tenth Amendment.

In the case of Weber vs. Doust, 146 Pac. 623, the Supreme Court of Washington said, "There is much fault in the general conception of liberty. Man in his natural state, has natural liberty if he has the physical power to maintain it. In his civil state, he must yield the natural right to obey his impulses to go to war at will to the social compact, whatever must be its form. In return society gives to all that subscribe to its norms a guarantee that it will protect him in those civil rights which by nature or by due ordination of law are recognized as essential to the health, peace and happiness of the greatest number." The facts of life in the nuclear age demand that we yield to the international socio-political compact—the UN—our impulses as nations to go to war at will.

In the case of Fitz Simmons vs. New York State Athletic Commission, 146 NYS 117, the Court said, "Liberty is a word with a double meaning. In a negative sense it secures freedom by the imposition of restraints. It is the positive sense that the state, in the exercise of its police and general welfare powers, promotes the freedom of all by the imposition of such restraints on some as are deemed necessary to the general welfare."

It was Daniel Webster in his famous speech before the South Carolina Bar Association who said: "Liberty exists in proportion of wholesome restraint," and it is our own Declaration of Independence that says, "All men . . . are endowed by their Creator with certain unalienable rights; that among these are life, liberty and the pursuit of happiness. That, to secure these rights, governments are instituted among men. . . ."

How is it possible then for man to live in freedom in his international society without the rule of law among nations and without the international imposition of restraints by an international authority? It is apparent that no individual or state within a nation can act without regard to the rights and welfare of other groups and individuals within the national society. How can we possibly have an ordered international society so long as each individual nation is permitted to pursue what it conceives to be its own welfare without restraint and regard for the rights and welfare of other nations and peoples? Is it not in fact this unbridled pursuit of national

self-interest that creates the chaotic international climate
that foments one international crisis after another?

But man is essentailly a social being; even in his savage
state, he recognizes that it is better to prescribe regulations
and restraints, though often crude and inadequate, than
for each man to be a law unto himself. These order-
ing forces have made it possible for individuals, families,
clans, tribes, communities and states within nations to live
together with some degree of harmony.

As men once separated by rivers banded together to
form nations, men today separated by the seas must now
join together to form a world government to bring to men
everywhere a new measure of freedom and morality. It
has been demonstrated beyond all doubt that pacts, coali-
tions, treaties, leagues, loose alliances and confederations
do not establish world peace. The government that is to
speak for all men must have the power commensurate
with its task of securing a just peace and elevating man
to a new level of freedom with justice under law.

National sovereignty like individual personal liberty
exists in proportion to wholesome restraints. It is the
failure to understand this truth that has led us to try to
protect our sovereignty with armies, navies and treaties.
These are not substitutes for government. It is the attempt to try to make this substitution that has caused our
nation to lose—not gain—sovereignty over the destiny of
its youth, its economy and the utilization of its natural
resources. If we are to regain this sovereignty; if we are
to resume our sovereignty over our resources, stop the
levy of confiscatory taxes and cease the conscription of our
young people, there must be an effective governing force
among nations to reflect the sovereign will of all men.
Law is potentially no less the instrument of peace and
freedom at the international level than at other levels of

man's society. As a nation our agreement to join with other nations to settle disputes by law would itself be the positive exercise of our national sovereignty. A lawless world is the great enemy of national sovereignty. To argue that the abolition of war would destroy national sovereignty is to argue that it is necessary to have war to maintain sovereignty. To recognize the fallacy of this argument, it is only necessary to imagine the chaos that would obtain should domestic sovereignty reign un-abridged with courts of law unavailable for the settlement of private controversies. In point of fact, it would be the supreme triumph of national sovereignty should it be exercised to bring a nation into a viable effective govern-mental arrangement with other nations to rid the world of international war and bring to the world community a new measure of freedom and dignity under law. As important as this triumph would be, the supervening consideration—the very reason for the creation of nations—is the sover-eignty of the individual. It is this sovereignty that would be served by a government of the whole. In some nations this would be considered of secondary importance to the triumph of national sovereignty, but the effect would be the same. Human beings throughout the world would be the benefactors regardless of the political philosophy of their homeland.

It is this sovereignty of the individual that should constitute the principal concern of Western nations. While government and law for the world would permit nations to regain sovereignty over their youth and natural re-sources, world government would, at the same time, secure to men of all lands a new status, a freedom of the individual heretofore unknown in the history of man's evolution.

No individual dedication could be more consonant with universal religious principles than that each of us commit himself to the elevation of the sovereignty and worth of the individual human being. Where the demands of national sovereignty seek to override the tenets of this precept such demands should be ignored. Where alleged national interests run counter to human interests they should not be countenanced. No nation or combination of nations deserves our first allegiance. Our first allegiance must be to the sovereignty of the human spirit. If this means—as it surely does—the creation of an adequate world authority to serve the worldwide human needs of our time, we must not be deterred from attaining this goal by those whose vision is beclouded by the current military demands of any nation or combination of nations. We must stop measuring our national sovereignty in megakills and begin to recover the personal freedoms and economic control of our natural resources which we have sacrificed to the war system. Such a recovery of lost sovereignty can be effected only through the establishment of an effective international structure of law and government.

"It is better to suffer injustice than to commit it."

—SOCRATES

PERSONAL MILITARY INVOLVEMENT

Since religious belief and training are a basis for exemption from military service in the United States, it is important to examine in some depth the provisions of our draft law, more formally known as the Universal Military Training and Service Act, with particular emphasis on those provisions therein which deal with the "conscientious objector."[1]

Conscientious objectors fall into three categories:

1. Those who object to combatant military service, but are willing to serve in army units defined as "non-combatant." Under the present law, such men are classified I-A-O. They are inducted in the same order and manner as regular inductees which are classed I-A, but I-A-O men are assigned only to non-combatant duty.

2. All those men opposed to military service both combatant and non-combatant. If their claims are sustained, they are classified as I-O and assigned to "civilian work contributing to the maintenance of the national health, safety or interest."

1. For an excellent discussion of this subject see: *Handbook for Conscientious Objectors*, Fifth Revised Edition, published by The Central Committee for Conscientious Objectors, 2006 Walnut Street, Philadelphia 3, Pennsylvania.

3. Those men who will accept neither military service nor any kind of alternative service under the conscription program. These men have been called "absolutists," and they frequently refuse to register or fill out the questionnaires or report for service. Generally they are subjected to criminal prosecution and imprisonment.

There are two national agencies that will advise conscientious objectors without charge. These are: The Central Committee of Conscientious Objectors, 2006 Walnut Street, Philadelphia 3, Pennsylvania, and the National Service Board for Religious Objectors, 401 Third Street, N.W., Washington 1, D.C. The former organization, the Central Committee, specializes in cases of men who face legal difficulties with Selective Service resulting from violations of the law or for those conscientious objectors who have had difficulty in classification due to the narrow religious "Supreme Being" requirements of the law. The National Service Board is better for dealing quickly with Selective Service on Presidential appeals.

The Universal Military Training and Service Act was approved by Congress on June 19, 1951 and was an amendment and extension of the Selective Service Act of 1948. Subsequent extensions of the Act were made in 1959 and 1963. It comes up for renewal again in 1967.

The Selective Service Act of 1948 was the first peacetime draft in our nation's history. While it has been amended and renamed, it retains its essential character as a program to conscript our youth in their most formative years for training in methods of warfare. With each extension of the draft, the vocal opposition decreases and it has for all intents and purposes become an accepted peacetime demand of our government on its citizens. This point is illustrated by the fact that the extension of the draft in 1963 to 1967 passed the house on a vote of 387 to 3 and was rushed through in ten minutes. This is not to say that the populace does not object to the peacetime draft, it has simply come to feel that opposition to it is useless as it seemingly has become an unalterable part of the scheme of things. They are told that the national security is involved, yet there is mounting evidence that the draft is disruptive of the nation's youth to the point of being a contributor to the problem of juvenile delinquency; that it is wasteful of our manpower resources, unneeded and in flagrant violation of our traditional concept of individual freedom in time of peace.

Title 50, Appendix Section 456 (j) of the Act says: "Nothing contained in this Title shall be construed to require any person to be subject to combatant training and service in the armed forces of the United States, who, by reasons of religious training and belief, is conscientiously opposed to participation in war in any form. Religious training and belief in this connection means an individual's belief in a relation to a Supreme Being involving duties superior to those arising from any human relation, but does not include essentially political, sociological, or philosophical views or a merely personal moral code. Any persons claiming exemption from combatant training and service because of such conscientious objection whose claim is sustained by the local board shall, if he is inducted into the armed forces under this title, be assigned to noncombatant service as defined by the President, or shall, if he is found to be conscientiously opposed to participation in such noncombatant service, in lieu of such induction, be ordered by his local board, subject to such regulations as the President may prescribe, to perform for a period equal to the period prescribed in Section 4 (b) [Section 454 (b) of this Appendix] such civilian work contributing to the maintenance of the national health, safety or interests as the local board may deem appropriate. . . ."

Section 462 of the Appendix says, ". . . any person . . . who evades or refuses registration or service in the armed forces or any of the requirements of this title, or who knowingly counsels, aids, or abets another to refuse or evade registration or service in the armed forces or any of the requirements of this title . . . or who in any manner shall knowingly fail or neglect or refuse to perform any duty required of him under or in execution of this title, or rules, regulations, or directions made pursuant to this title, or any person or persons who shall knowingly hinder or interfere or attempt to do so in any way, by force, or violence or otherwise, with the administration of this title . . . shall upon conviction in any district court of the United States . . . be punished by imprisonment for not more than five years or a fine of not more than $10,000.00 or both such fine and imprisonment. . . ."

Since an offense punishable by death or imprisonment for a term greater than one year is a felony, and since persons convicted of felonies under the federal law lose voting and other civil rights and privileges in some states, a Presidential pardon would generally be required for civil rights and privileges to be restored to one who has been convicted of a violation of the Act.[2]

The person desiring conscientious classification must request on his initial draft questionnaire that he be sent Form No. 150. This form is mailed to all registrants who sign the Conscientious Objection paragraph on their Classification Questionnaire.

The Conscientious Objector's Form is divided into Five series: In Series I, the applicant indicates whether or not he wishes non-combatant service in the armed forces or

2. Federal Code Annotated 18, Section 1.

strictly civilian service. Under Series II, there are seven questions. The first one is: "Do you believe in a Supreme Being?" A "yes" or "no" answer is required. The second question asks the registrant to set forth the nature of his belief in a Supreme Being and to state whether or not his belief involves duties which are to him superior to those arising from any human relations.[3] Question number three asks the registrant to explain from whom and from what source he received his training and belief. Question number four requires him to give the name and present address of the individual upon whom he relies most for religious guidance. Number five asks under what circumstances, if any, does the registrant believe in the use of force. In connection with this question, it is often asked at induction hearings, "What would you do if someone tried to rape your wife?" In question number six, the applicant is asked to describe the actions and behavior in his life which in his opinion most conspicuously demonstrates the consistency and depth of his religious conviction, and number seven asks if the applicant has ever given public expression either written or oral to his views.

Series III of the questionnaire deals with the general background of the applicant, his education and occupation.

Series IV concerns the organizations in which the applicant has participated. If he has ever been a member of a military organization he must explain fully why he has now changed his views. In one question the applicant is asked to describe carefully the creed or official statement

3. It should be noted here that the cases of Taffs v. U.S., 208 F2d 329; U.S. v. Hartman, 209 F2d 366; Jesson v. U.S. 212 F2d 897; and Sicurella v. U.S., 348 U.S. 385, indicate that it is not sufficient to object to some types of war although it is not a bar to conscientious objector classification if one is willing to participate in a theocratic war or use force in self-defense. See also; U.S. v. Hertzog, 122 F. Supp. 632 and Bouziden v. U.S., 251 F2d 728.

of his religious sect in relation to participation in war. It should be noted here that membership in a church is not required for recognition as a conscientious objector.

Finally, Series V deals with references; one must state those—for example, parents, ministers, teachers—who personally know of his conscientious objector beliefs.

Notice of Classification

When a registrant gets his Notice of Classification he may file a written request for a hearing within ten days. The local board has the authority to permit someone to appear before it on behalf of the registrant, but it is very clear that no registrant can demand as a matter of right to be represented before the local board by anyone acting as his attorney or legal counsel or otherwise in his behalf.[4] The draft board is supposed to post a list of Advisors to Registrants, but the courts have held that a failure to do so does not per se constitute a denial of due process.[5]

Appeal From Classification

Within ten days after the first notice of classification, the registrant may file notice of appeal. In addition to the registrant, an appeal may be taken by a government agent attached to each local board or by a person claiming to be a dependent of the registrant or by an employer who, prior to classification, has filed a written request for deferment of the registrant. This appeal is to the Appeal Board. If this board refuses his lower classification request or makes a tentative determination in his behalf, the

4. Executive order No. 9988, 13 F.R. 4851 Part 624.1 (August 20, 1948). Title 32, Sec. 1624.1 (b).

5. Clark v. U.S. 236 F2d 13, Code of Federal Regulations; Title 32, Section 1604.41.

registrant's file is sent to the Department of Justice for an advisory recommendation.

Department of Justice Hearing

The Department of Justice then routinely has the FBI investigate the case. Agents of the FBI interview many people who know the registrant. The FBI report is forwarded to a hearing officer appointed by the Department of Justice. The hearing officer notifies the registrant of the time and place of his hearing. The hearing officer after the hearing makes a recommendation to the Department of Justice as to whether or not the registrant should be classified as a conscientious objector. The Department of Justice in turn sends an advisory recommendation to the Appeal Board stating why it finds the registrant's conscientious objector claim should not be sustained. A copy of this recommendation is sent to the registrant with a letter informing him that he has thirty days in which to file a reply to the Department of Justice recommendation. The Appeal Board then classifies the registrant in the lowest class for which it feels him eligible. The report of the Department of Justice is only advisory and the Appeal Board does not have to accept the recommendation contained therein. The Appeal Board neither sees the registrant nor sees the full FBI report. The registrant is given a hearing before the Department of Justice, but he does not see the FBI file nor does he know the nature of the evidence used against him, nor does he know the names of the informers whom the FBI men have questioned.[6] Thus, he is then helpless to protect himself against malicious and untrue information which may be in his file.[7]

6. Clark v. U.S., 126 F2d 13.
7. U.S. v. DeRemer, 221 F. Supp. 553.

The registrant may be represented by an advisor at the hearing held by the Department of Justice and he may take witnesses with him. But the advisor may not represent the registrant in the usual legal sense. There can be no argument and no objecting to questions. The proceeding is largely in the hands of the hearing officer. The hearing officer may ask any of a wide range of questions such as: "What would you do if you saw your wife criminally attacked?" A report of this Department of Justice hearing goes to the Appeal Board and has great influence on the Board as it makes its final determination as to the classification to be given the registrant. In spite of the importance of this report, only a summary thereof is placed in the registrant's file.

Final Determination of Classification

The Director of Selective Service or the State Director may order the Appeal Board to reconsider its determination if they "deem it to be in the national interest or necessary to avoid any injustices," but after the Appeal Board has finally acted the last avenue for a change of classification open to the registrant—if an adverse classification has been received—is to appeal directly to the President. If the decision of the Appeal Board was unanimous, the registrant cannot personally appeal, but even in these circumstances an appeal can be taken by the National or State Director of Selective Service, if either deems it would be "in the national interest or necessary to avoid an injustice." As a practical matter, it is extremely difficult to get the State or National Director to take such an appeal. As previously indicated, the National Service Board for Religious Objectors (see Appendix D of this volume) can be of assistance in securing a presidential review of the registrant's classification.

No registrant may be inducted after any of the preceding appeals have been granted and are pending, but efforts to get an appeal do not stop induction proceedings. Induction is not postponed even while the registrant is attempting to get the State or National Director to take a presidential appeal. The finding of the Presidential Appeal Board is the basis for a new notice of classification to the registrant and a statement relative to the findings of the Board is placed in the Selective Service file of the registrant.

Civilian Work For The Conscientious Objector

A registrant classified as I-O is assigned to civilian work. Under the law civilian work is (*1*) employment by the United States government, or by a state, territory, or possession of the United States or by a political subdivision thereof, or by the District of Columbia, (*2*) employment by a nonprofit organization, association or corporation which is primarily engaged either in a charitable activity conducted for the benefit of the general public or in carrying out a program for the improvement of public health or welfare, including educational and scientific activities in support thereof, when such activity or program is not principally for the benefit of the members of such organization, association, or corporation, or for increasing the membership thereof.[8]

The Act specifically rules out private employment other than by an approved non-profit organization;[9] the I-O registrant works the same hours, receives the same pay and vacation and is otherwise subject to the same conditions as other employees on the same job. He can be discharged as other employees and, if this is done, he is

8. Code of Federal Regulations; Title 32, Section 1660.1 (a).
9. Code of Federal Regulations; Title 32, Section 1660.1 (b).

supposed to secure the same type of work with some other employer.

The registrant may submit his choice of the type of civilian work he prefers to his local board and before a mandatory work order is issued to the I-O registrant the board must secure him a job, but not necessarily of the type preferred by the registrant. Only if the registrant refuses to report for this assigned work and fails to respond to this work order do the criminal provisions of the law go into effect. If he refuses to report, he will face prosecution in the United States District Court having jurisdiction over the place where the civilian work is to be performed.[10]

As a practical matter, I-O registrants are not usually assigned to work in their home communities, but this may be done if the local board deems it "to be desirable in the national interest." There is no assurance that the I-O registrant will even be assigned to work in the United States.

After twenty-four months of service in civilian work has been completed, the conscientious objector will be sent a certificate of release from civilian work and classified "I-W Released." The two years of civilian work required of the I-O registrant is figured from the effective date of the order to report for civilian work.

After Classification Has Been Completed

After classification has been completed and the war objector finds himself in Class I-A or I-A-O, he is then subject to the order to report for induction. At this point his remaining remedy lies in defending himself in the courts by attacking the Selective Service order in his case

10. Johnson v. U.S., 351 U.S. 215.

as illegal. The registrant may refuse to report for induction or refuse to be inducted. In either case his name will be reported to the Attorney General and arrest will follow. While the Selective Service Act states that the decisions of the local and appeals boards shall be final, the Supreme Court has held that limited judicial review is possible.[11]

The majority of acquittals are won in those cases where it can be shown to the satisfaction of the court that the Selective Service Act was not followed and procedural errors in the handling of the case were made. This is well set forth by the court in U.S. v. Zieber, 161 F2d 90 (1947). In this case the court said, "good faith and honest intention on the part of the local board is not enough. There must be full and fair compliance with the provisions of the Act and the applicable regulations."

Should a registrant be acquitted in the criminal court, then his classification is reopened with opportunities to add to his file, appeal any subsequent classification and to have new hearings.

Treatment of the Objector

During World War II, more than 6,000 conscientious objectors were sentenced to federal prison by United States District Courts. About two thirds of these were Jehovah's Witnesses.

11. In the case of Gibson v. U.S. and Dobez v. U.S. in 329 U.S. 33 decided in 1946 the Court said, "provided that he has exhausted his administrative remedies, the registrant who has not been actually inducted in the armed forces may in defense of a criminal prosecution attack a board's order as arbitrary and illegal." It seems clear, however, from the case of Cox v. U.S. 332 U.S. 442 that no intervention or interference by the courts will be made unless the action of the local board was not in conformity with the regulations of the Selective Service Act or where their action was "shockingly arbitrary." Dickinson v. U.S. 346 U.S. 389 and subsequent cases.

The convicted registrant is handcuffed and taken by the federal marshal to a county jail where he waits a matter of a few days to a few weeks following sentencing at which time he is taken to a federal prison. At federal prison he undergoes a ten to fifteen minute interview by psychiatrists, who then proceed to write a sweeping diagnosis about the prisoner. This diagnosis often follows a standard form for conscientious objectors, e.g., mother fixation, antipathy for father, sexual maladjustments, latent homosexuality, etc.

At Christmas time each inmate receives a brown paper sack containing hard candy and cigarettes. He may write letters—three a week—each letter not more than one page in length. All letters are censored, both those coming in and going out.

His assignment will fall into one of some five different prison work categories: (*1*) maintenance jobs within the institution; (*2*) industrial jobs connected with whatever project the particular institution may be participating, (*3*) work on the prison farm; (*4*) ditch digging and other "made jobs" which absorb the surplus of the prison labor force and; (*5*) office or administrative jobs, such as secretarial work in the parole office, work in the library or chaplain's office. These are regarded as the soft jobs, but some C.O.'s have refused to take these jobs because of the involvement in the administration of the prison.

The federal prisoner is subject to parole after he serves one-third of his sentence. An inmate serving a sentence longer than six months can get "good time" which is deducted from the length of his sentence. The amount deducted is five days per month on a sentence of six months to one year, six days per month on a sentence of one year to three years, seven days per month on a sentence from over three years to five years.

Religion Sole Basis for Conscientious Objector Classification

Since Series II of the questionnaire contains seven questions relative to the objector's religion, it is interesting to determine what the word "religion" means in the Selective Service System. As has been noted, the regular classification questionnaire which is sent to each registrant by Selective Service Department's local board contains a statement which is to be signed by those who wish to have a special conscientious objector form sent to them. This application statement says, "By reasons of religious training and belief I am conscientiously opposed to participation in war in any form and for this reason hereby request that the local board furnish me a Special Form for Conscientious Objectors (SSS Form 150) which I am to complete and return to the local board for its consideration."

In the case of In re. Nissen, 146 F. Supp. 361, November 20, 1956, at page 363, the Court said, "So far as Congress was thinking of 'training' it regarded it as meaning no more than individual experience supporting belief; a mere background against which sincerity would be tested." In the case of United States v. Horst, Criminal Document 36149 (E.D.S. Michigan), December 2, 1957, the United States District Court from Michigan has used the definition of religious training and belief, or rather interpreted the meaning of religion as used in the Act to mean "any belief, orthodox or unorthodox." The Court also held that Congress did not intend that the registrant's claim of exemption carry with it any special concept of fear or religious sanctions, such as punishment after death or excommunication.

Section V (j) of the Selective Training and Service Act of 1940 said, "Nothing contained in this act shall be

construed to require any person to be subject to combatant training and service in the land or naval forces of
the United States, who, by reason or religious training
and belief, is conscientiously opposed to participation in
war in any form."

Again, Section VI (j) of the present law reads much
the same but continues from there as follows: "Religious
training and belief in this connection means an individual's
belief in relation to the Supreme Being involving duties
superior to those arising from any human relation, but does
not include essentially political, sociological, or philosophical views or a merely personal moral code." In 283
U.S. 605, the MacIntosh case, Justice Hughes wrote
relative to the meaning of the required belief in a Supreme Being: "The essence of religion is belief in a relation to God involving duties superior to those arising
from any human relation." It is to be noted that this is
almost the same definition as used in the language of the
statute. But it should be remembered that a person who
objects to war on other than religious basis, i.e., whose
objection is not based on religious training and belief, is
specifically eliminated by law from consideration for
classification as a conscientious objector.

The Use of Force Factor

Question five on Form 150 asks the objector, "Under
what circumstances, if any, do you believe in the use of
force?"

On the use of force, the local board may question
the conscientious objector applicant as follows: "Didn't
the United Nations carry out police action in Korea?"
"Wouldn't you stop a maniac from killing you?" "Would
you stop a maniac from killing himself?" "Would you use
force to restrain a child from rushing into danger?"

"Didn't Jesus use violence in driving the money-changers from the temple?" "Would you force medical treatment upon a delirious patient?" "Would you use force to keep a little girl from being molested?" "Would you use force to stop someone from killing your mother?" These are some of the questions that have been asked by the local boards of conscientious objectors, albeit they are irrelevant to the question of force used in international warfare.

The decision on how to classify a registrant made by the classifying personnel hinges in large measure on the draft board's disposition toward the applicant for conscientious objection status and his sincerity of conviction.

It is important to remember that a conscientious objector does not have to object to the use of force of every kind to receive a non-military or non-combatant classification. Whether or not a registrant who opposes war but not international police action would be classified as a conscientious objector would depend on the classification personnel involved in his particular case; probably the registrant would not find official sympathy for such a distinction unless he could relate it to his religious belief and training.

The Philosophy of the Non-Registrant

As has been previously observed, anyone qualified for induction who refuses to register for the draft or to co-operate with Selective Service is subject to imprisonment. Why would a young man prefer prison?

The statement of a young married college graduate with two children, who had his education interrupted twice for refusal to co-operate with the Selective Service System, is of interest. A portion of his statement relative to the action he took is as follows:

"The Selective Service System itself can be reason enough for a non-registrant's objections. Its narrow definition of a conscientious objector excludes those who might object to war on other than strictly religious grounds. The draft and appeal boards act as judges of whether one's religious convictions are sincere or not. Sometimes unfair and arbitrary decisions are made by them.

"It seems to me that a conscientious objector, operating within the Selective Service law, is still a part of the total picture of the preparation for war. It is expedient, even though done with reluctance, for the government to recognize a conscientious objector and then put him aside in civilian service, meanwhile continuing to conscript other men to learn to kill. I cannot be a part of a system that conscripts other men to kill, even though they do not object to it.

"To be most effective, the non-registrant's stand must arise out of a way of life in which a seemingly negative attitude actually is a confirmation of the well-integrated spirit. It may be that this refusal to co-operate with Selective Service is the only way he can continue to live by those principles in which he believes. A sensitive person co-operates with most of the laws of man. It is his duty to abide by those laws which are not contrary to his conscience. It is also his responsibility to oppose, by refusing to co-operate with, those laws which violate his conscience."[12]

Conclusion

Somewhere between the philosophy expressed by this young man and that of the professional soldier lies the

12. See *Positions of Conscientious Objectors*, a synopsis, Friends' Peace Committee, 1520 Race Street, Philadelphia 2, Pennsylvania.

view of the average man—the young American—the mass
of our draft-age youth. They are the confused, the be-
wildered, who in their most formative period face the
inevitable decision of what to do about the draft. Most
of these youngsters want to do what is best for their country; many realize that their country's best interests lie in
a viable, peaceful relationship with other nations. They
believe in law and government at the local, state and national level because they have been reared in that tradition. World government has probably not been considered by them because of a lack of emphasis in their educational background, but lawlessness, mass destruction and
murder are abhorrent to their thinking. They do not wish
to engage in these practices at the international level of
their society any more than they would engage in these
practices in their home towns. Parents, church and press
often attempt to justify war, but such efforts are generally something less than satisfying persuasive to these
young people.

The Constitution of the United States, states that
"Neither slavery nor involuntary servitude, except as a
punishment for crime whereof the party shall have been
duly convicted, shall exist within the United States, or any
place subject to their jurisdiction."[13]

Does the draft law violate the Constitution by forc-
ing young men into the military under penalty of imprisonment and loss of citizenship? The courts to date
have said it does not, but these holdings must fail to impress those who have known the absolute and unquestioning
servitude demanded of draftees by the military. In the
Niles case,[14] the court said the Thirteenth Amendment
was not intended to limit the "war powers of government

13. Thirteenth Amendment, Section 1.
14. U.S. v. Niles, 122 F. Supp. 382.

or its right to exact by law public service from all to meet
the public need," quoting with approval from an earlier
case.[15]

But what are the limits of this power? Should it extend to peacetime conscription? A peacetime draft had
never been used in this country at the time the Thirteenth
Amendment was enacted. The words of the amendment
are not restricted to the abolition of slavery, but say
"neither slavery nor involuntary servitude" shall exist.[16]
Was the government itself to be restricted by the amendment? Obviously so, as the lone exception dealt with the
government and its right to punish for crime those who
"shall have been duly convicted." It strains the reason of
the most credulous citizen to ask him to believe that it is not
involuntary servitude to present to a young man the choice
of being drafted or going to a federal penitentiary.

Does the right to "raise and support armies" granted
the Congress mean that it has the right to draft a man
against his will in peacetime? In the Etcheverry case,[17]
the court held that the peacetime draft is justified by the
power granted Congress to "raise armies" and, too, that
a citizen's right not to be deprived of his liberty without
due process of law is not violated when he is inducted
pursuant to the provisions of the draft law.

Is it due process not to present an objecting registrant
the reasons for his classification? The courts have held
that due process is not thereby violated.[18] Is it a deprivation of due process to require a man to enter military
service and not allow him to examine the FBI-garnered
evidence on which he was classified? No, according to the
case of Bouziden v. U.S., 251 Fed. 2d 728.

15. Heflin v. Sanford, 142 F2d 798.
16. U.S. Constitution, Article 1, Section 8 (12).
17. Etcheverry v. U.S., 320 F2d 873.
18. Osburn v. U.S. 319 F2d 915.

All of these pronouncements by the federal courts upholding the constitutionality of the peacetime draft law and the procedures it directs are extremely strained and unconvincing. These cases represent the dogmatic holdings of judges who have arbitrarily found that the right to "raise and support armies" means the right to conscript and underpay and that the phrase "involuntary servitude" does not encompass one who is forced under penalty of imprisonment and loss of citizenship to enter the military forces.

There is no doubt that in the past men of deep faith and fundamental objection to war and to military service have had their freedom arbitrarily taken from them under the powers of the draft act. For them due process has been theory, not a practicality. They have been impressed into the military to perform involuntary service for which they have received only token remuneration. If the federal government can "exact by law public service from all to meet the public need"[19] then civilian workers, who are as vital to the military as soldiers, may one day be involuntarily conscripted in peacetime to perform in the public interest.

Mention should be made of the case of U.S. v. Bortlik, 122 F. Supp. 225, relative to the requirement that a conscientious objector be opposed to "war in any form." In this case the registrant said he was not a pacifist but a "servant of God." He further stated that he would be willing to use force and to fight if God revealed to him that such was his duty. The court held that this qualification to the registrant's objection to war did not per se remove him from consideration for conscientious objector classification by his draft board.

19. *Ibid.*

In reaching its conclusions, the court felt it needed to
define "war" as used in the draft law. The court said
war "is a conflict by force between two or more nations;
it is a conflict of violence by one politically organized
body seeking to overcome or overthrow another political
entity. It is patent Congress was legislating in regard to
this type of struggle. . . ."

Clearly, United Nations police action as exemplified
by its presence in various parts of the world does not constitute "war" within the court's definition. The UN is
not a country, but represents a composite of world opinion;
its purpose in sending troops to world trouble spots is
not to "overthrow or overcome another political entity"
but to quell and prevent the rise of armed force; to stand
between opposing nations for the good of all nations.
United Nations military action is not directed to the overthrow of governments, but to their protection. This
clearly distinguishes UN police action from unilateral
or multilateral international warfare.

Hopefully, the federal government will make provision for those young people who make this distinction
and who could in good conscience serve in a UN police
unit, but find service in a national army at variance with
their faith.

For the young men who desire to serve in the maintenance of world peace through service to the United Nations, our nation should enter an agreement with the UN
pursuant to Article 43 (1) of the Charter whereby we
create an armed force to be placed at the disposal of the
Security Council. Service in this unit would be service on
behalf of all mankind. This unit would be subject to use
arms only after being so directed by the Security Council
or by the General Assembly in the event the Security
Council is prevented from acting by the veto in matters

affecting world peace.[20] It would be in essence a world police force unit.

The consummation of such an agreement with the United Nations would not only serve what will become an increasingly larger segment of our young citizenry, but would be a great leading step by our great nation toward re-establishing its image and prestige abroad as the "home of the free."

There is a case that hopefully may herald the beginning of the end of strained and contorted judicial reasoning that has glossed over fundamental abuses to the rights of the man of faith who finds the military incompatible with his beliefs.

In U.S. v. Seeger, 326 F2d 846, the defendant had appealed from a lower court decision finding him guilty of refusing to submit to induction into the armed forces.

Judge Kaufman writing the opinion found that the statute limiting the conscientious objection exemption from military service to persons who believe in a Supreme Being violates the due process clause of the Fifth Amendment by creating an impermissible classification as applied to one whose abhorrence to war is sincere and is predicated on religious training and belief.

The government conceded that Seeger's abhorrence to war was sincere and predicated on "religious training and belief." (See U.S. v. Kauten, 133 F 2d 703).

He did not on his first application to his board claim to be a conscientious objector. He later wrote a letter to his board stating his conscientious objector views. He

20. Article 43 (1) says: "All members of the United Nations, in order to contribute to the maintenance of international peace and security, undertake to make available to the Security Council, on its call and in accordance with a special agreement or agreements, armed forces, assistance and facilities, including rights of passage, necessary for the purpose of maintaining international peace and security."

further elaborated his views when his board sent him the conscientious objector form. On the form he placed quotes around the word "religious" and deleted the words "training and" from the printed oath he was to sign on the conscientious objector form. He added, that "Such personages as Plato, Aristotle and Spinoza evolved comprehensive ethical systems of intellectual and moral integrity without belief in God, except in the remotest sense." He went on to say that "the existence of God cannot be proven or disproven, and the essence of His nature cannot be determined. I prefer to admit this, and leave the question open rather than answer 'yes' or 'no.'" He added that his "skepticism or disbelief in the existence of God does not necessarily mean lack of faith in anything whatsoever. . . ." Seeger asserted that he had a "belief in and devotion to goodness and virtue for their own sakes, and a religious faith in a purely ethical creed." To underscore further his position, he decried "the tremendous price that man pays for his willingness to resort to mass destruction of human life to perpetuate his 'ideals.'" "I cannot, Seeger contended, "participate in actions which betray the cause of freedom and humanity. Experience with the past indicates that our armament policy will lead to war, and war, with its indiscriminate crushing of human personality, cannot preserve moral values. . . . To resort to immoral means is not to preserve or vindicate moral values, but only to become collaborators in destroying all moral life among men."

His board was unmoved and he was classified I-A and ordered to take a pre-induction physical. He personally appeared before the board to no avail. He sought review by the Appeal Board which routinely sent his file to the Department of Justice for an advisory opinion.

They in turn requested the FBI to investigate the accuracy and sincerity of Seeger's claims.

A resumé of the FBI report was forwarded to a hearing officer of the Department of Justice, hearing was held and Seeger with two witnesses appeared. The Hearing Officer reported that he was impressed with Seeger and found him sincere in his claims to have the beliefs he had set forth in his written statements to the draft board. The Hearing Officer recommended the appeal be sustained, but the Justice Department advised against allowing Seeger an exemption since his beliefs were not based on a "belief in a relation to a Supreme Being" as required by the U.S. Code. The Appeal Board, presumably for the same reason, voted to uphold his I-A classification.

Seeger thereupon refused to report for induction and prosecution and conviction ensued. The court found that in order to perfect his appeal it was necessary that he take all steps required of him short of final submission to induction in order to challenge "constitutional infirmities" in the jurisdiction of the draft law that denied him exemption.

During World War I the Draft Act of 1917, 40 Stat. 78, permitted exemption for conscientious objectors only if they were affiliated with a "well-recognized religious sect or organization at present organized and existing and whose existing creed or principles forbid its members to participate in war in any form."

The conscientious objector provisions of the 1940 Selective Service Act were broader in scope. This act, in effect throughout World War II, exempted from combat training any person "who by reason of religious training and belief, is conscientiously opposed to participation in war in any form."

The courts were subsequently called upon to define "religion" as used in the statute, and Augustus Hand in U.S. v. Kauten, 133 F2d 703 wrote: "Religious belief arises from a sense of inadequacy of reason as a means of relating the individual to his fellowman and to his universe—a sense common to men in the most primitive and in the most highly civilized societies. It accepts the aid of logic but refuses to be limited by it. It is a belief finding expression in a conscience which categorically requires the believer to disregard elementary self-interest and to accept martydom in preference to transgressing its tenets. Recognition of this obligation moved the Greek poet Menander to write almost twenty-four hundred years ago: 'Conscience is a God to all mortals,' impelled Socrates to obey the voice of his 'Daimon' and led Wordsworth to characterize 'Duty' as the 'Stern Daughter of the Voice of God.' "

It was in 1948 that the Congress inserted the requirement that a citizen must have a "belief in a relation to a Supreme Being" as a pre-requisite for exemption from military service.

In the Seeger case, the court also said ". . . we feel compelled to recognize that a requirement of belief in a Supreme Being, no matter how crudely defined, cannot embrace all those faiths which can validly claim to be called 'religious'. Thus, it has been noted that, among other well-established religious sects, Buddhism, Taoism, Ethical Culture and Secular Humanism do not teach belief in the existence of a Supreme Being" (citing Torcaso v. Watkins, 367 U.S. 488). The court recognized that ". . . today, a pervading commitment to a moral ideal is for many the equivalent of what was historically considered the response to divine commands." The finding of the court: ". . . Congress, in a sincere attempt to balance the personal rights of a minority with the insistent demands of national security, has transgressed the limits inforced by the Constitution. . . ."

There was inconsistency between the due process clause of the Fifth Amendment and the requirement of belief in a Supreme Being too great to be allowed to stand. To hold otherwise would, the court reasoned, be to discriminate against those citizens of equal conviction and religious sincerity who either did not believe in a Supreme Being or who were unsure of His existence in their own minds. In addition, the Supreme Being clause clearly discriminated against those of firm religious training and belief whose religions were not theistic. (In this regard it is appropriate to note that in interpreting the word "religion" as applied to organizations seeking tax exempt status, two courts have held the word "religion" can include groups possessing no theistic beliefs within the meaning of the law.)[21]

It can be hoped that future judicial decisions will continue in this manner to exempt from military service those who from deep conviction cannot engage in military activities.

No Future Need For Draft

This is an age of highly mobile, technically skilled military units. The emphasis is no longer on numbers. At the same time, there are more men of draft age than ever before. Each year over 1.8 million men in the U.S. reach eighteen years of age, but only 100,000 of them are required to fill the demands of the military. Why, then,

21. Fellowship of Humanity v. County of Alameda; 153 Col. App. 2d 673, 315 P2d 394; Washington Ethical Society v. District of Columbia, 101 U.S. App. D.C. 371, 249 F2d 127.

disrupt the lives of nearly two million men to select 100,-
000?

We could easily attract this required number of
eighteen-year-olds by adequate pay and other incentives
which is their due. This also holds for each of the other
draft age groups. Aside from all constitutional questions,
the military needs can be met without the peacetime draft
and without the frustrating and debasing effect it has on
our nation and its youth.

Each year only 40 to 48 per cent of the men reaching
twenty-six years of age in the U.S. have served in the
armed forces. Thus, the Act is hardly "universal" as its
name would imply. Of those who are drafted, only 2.8
per cent re-enlist; 97.2 per cent get out of the military as
quickly as they can. The money (at least $18,000 per
individual) spent for their training is, then, in large measure wasted. More incentives made available to these
men would encourage many of them to remain in the
armed forces. At the same time, increased pay and opportunity for military personnel generally would attract
men displaced by industrial automation to seek military
careers.

With decreased need for manpower in industry, with
an increase in the number of men reaching draft age,
with added incentives to enlist and re-enlist, the military
draft can and should be abandoned as unwanted and unneeded.

UNITY AMID DIVERSITY

While there are unquestionably differences between all human beings and their social groupings, there are undeniable basic similarities as well. To understand the full importance of these similarities it is helpful to look into the field of embryology and to begin at the very moment of conception of a human being.

All people regardless of their race or national origin belong to the species homo sapiens. What we are at birth is determined by genes in the germ plasm of our parents, our parents passing to us some of the characteristics of our forebears. This contribution of our ancestors to what we are is very revealing. If each of us were to trace our lineage back twenty generations, we would find more than a million ancestors each of whom has contributed in some measure to our genetic makeup. Pursued further, we would find that there is an actual kinship between all human beings. The phrase "brotherhood of man" then in fact has significant scientific support as well as religious emphasis.

It was believed until relatively recent times that man was created spontaneously. In the fourth century B.C., Aristotle, who wrote the first known treatise on embryology, concluded that a child was progressively generated out of its mother's menstrual blood. It was not until 1668, when Francesco Redi experimented with maggots growing in decaying meat, that it was demonstrated that life does not generate spontaneously. His conclusions were supported later by the work of Pasteur and Tyndall. Thus was born the concept that life is created from pre-existing organisms. How this is done was the subject of investigation by Oscar Hertwig, who in 1875 discovered the process of fertilization. The apparent kinship of different vertebrate embryos was later demonstrated by the scientists von Baer and Balfour. Scientists today in the field of embryology are aware that there is great unity among the life of the world. Each new life is made up of the very substance of the universe. Man, as a physical being, is a part of the stream of life in which elements of the universe are assembled in living form at conception and disassembled after death only to be reassembled and born again at a later time and into another life.

A human embryo reveals a yolk sac suggesting reptilian ancestors, a notochord similar to that of the earliest vertebrates, and a vestigial tail reminding us of our pre-human forebears. We also have vestigial gills—a linkage with the ages in which the forerunner of modern man spent in the sea.

The time man has been on this earth is relatively short. There is no assurance that he will survive in the ages to come. Man's existence on this earth has been but a scant few seconds in the day of time. There have been forms of life that preceded ours which inhabited the earth for a longer period than has man but who have now become extinct; their extinction having resulted from their inability to adjust to environmental change. Is man now to follow these extinct species into oblivion because he can not adjust to his changing environment?

For what purpose does man inhabit the earth? Are we here simply to outdo in violence and killing our pre-historic animal forebears and to direct our energies and substance to methods of self-destruction? Man can adjust, live and elevate his kind by agreeing to create the necessary world structure of law and government to control the devices of destruction which he has discovered or he can destroy his species. It is now within his power to do either.

If man is more than a physical form, and surely this is the case, he must not be guided by those who would be animal-like and divisive in their approach to his problems. To be deterred from the attainment of social justice by those who would wall us in behind a barrier of fear is to dedicate ourselves to the physical while denying the universality in the creation of man, his universal needs, rights and kinship. It is, most fundamentally, to deny to man the spirituality that differentiates him from the beasts of the field and lifts him out of the stream of physical life and places him on the mountain with his Creator.

Interestingly enough, there is found in practically all religous belief—be it atheistic as is Buddhism or theistic as is Christianity, Judaism and Islam—the concept that a unity that operates universally pervades the cosmic order. It can be said that the universality of man—his physical and spiritual kinship—is a matter of fact recognized by theologians and scientists throughout the world.

Again, the concept of the brotherhood of man is not a meaningless phrase, but one that has both deep scientific and spiritual roots. There indeed does exist a kinship among all men. Artificial barriers such as national boundaries, religion and economic philosophy in no way impair or nullify this basic truth. Needless to say, the

teachings of Jesus Christ and other great religious prophets and teachers are consistent with this reality.

If we as individuals are to differentiate ourselves
from the other vertebrae and lend substance to our claim
of spirituality, if we are to bear true allegiance to our
respective faiths and to ourselves, we must be concerned
with the burdens of our fellow man wherever he may be.
It would be a mockery to fail to have this concern and
to lay claim to any fundamental distinction from any
other species of animal life that inhabits the earth. We,
in effect, have a choice: we can live a material life un-
mindful of universal need or we can live with an awareness of man's burdens and at least in some measure serve
those fundamental needs of all men. It will be in direct
proportion to the extent of this service to man that we
serve our basic religious faiths and lay the necessary foundation for personal and national survival in the nuclear
age.

It is difficult to believe that man in his quiet moments
and during periods of personal stress and danger does
not understand in his heart his kinship to all life and his
duty to it. This truth is not constantly uppermost in
man's mind because he becomes distracted with day-to-day
concerns of personal comfort, sex, the form of religion,
gaiety, gadgetry and money. Our concern for the welfare of our brothers throughout the world tends to diminish in direct proportion to what appears to be our immediate national interests. For example, while it is true
that massive foreign aid has been sent abroad from our
shores, it is obvious that the concern has all too frequently
been political and military expediency rather than human
welfare, reflecting economic rather than humanistic concern. There is mounting evidence that this policy has not
served our nation well as resentment of us mounts as we

increasingly encumber our foreign aid with political and military involvements in the internal affairs of other nations.

If there is then a basic kinship or brotherhood which must be universally served as our primary duty, what are these universal needs and rights basic to all men that should constitute the goals of this service? The Universal Declaration of Human Rights and the summary of the Code of Offenses against the Peace and Security of Mankind which appear in the appendixes to this volume give expression to human rights and offenses against mankind that had their geneses in the emergence of man as a civilized creature.

The twentieth century is the most murderous and bloodiest century in all the preceding twenty-five centuries of Greco-Roman and Western history, when measured in terms of numbers killed in wars, revolutions, riots, and crimes per 1,000,000 of the world's inhabitants. This has come to pass because the military perversions of nations have not been subject to the restraint of the conscience of mankind. There has been a tragic misconception that national interests are human interests. The public conscience is mobilized and placed in effect through law and government. World law and government are now required to restrain nations from a continuation of their homicidal mischief.

If governments are instituted among men to secure to them the blessings of liberty—and this is the premise on which our national government was founded—is it not then tragic that there is not a democratic government at the world level of man's society to act for him in matters of universal concern?

It is ironic that those often loudest in their verbal championship of the cause of freedom are in the forefront of movements to circumscribe the activities and powers of the United Nations. It is frequently these self-styled "patriots" who stand in staunch opposition to measures to relieve suffering in foreign countries; who support the status quo in foreign lands against independence movements; who oppose the extension of the world rule of law and who generally associate international concern with anti-Americanism. What a tragedy that these people have purloined the word "patriot" from the language. If patriotism means dedication to the preservation and promotion of those ideals and high purpose for which this country was once dedicated, surely it is the man who believes in erecting a framework of government within which human rights can be secured to all men that constitutes the true patriot of our time. Democratic governments exist for people and are so created. Governments should be the tools of the people. Government for government's sake is worse than no government, and patriotism which amounts to government worship is idolatry in its most dangerous form. We must now shift our primary social allegiance from nations to mankind.

Since the rights of all men are universal and basic in their geneses and, since democratic government is the most effective instrument devised by man to secure these rights, and, since there are now matters of universal concern without the control of any nation, it is then logically compelling that democratic government be instituted at the world level of man's society if we are to secure the blessings of liberty and justice to all mankind in the nuclear age.

From the Master of Life, who made you.
　"I have given you lands to hunt in,
I have given you streams to fish in,
I have given you bear and bison,
I have given you roe and reindeer,
I have given you brant and beaver,
Filled the marshes full of wild-fowl,
Filled the rivers full of fishes;
Why then are you not contented?
Why then will you hunt each other?
　"I am weary of your quarrels,
Weary of your wars and bloodshed,
Weary of your prayers for vengeance,
Of your wranglings and dissensions;
All your strength is in your union,
All your danger is in discord;
Therefore be at peace henceforward,
And as brothers live together."

—HENRY W. LONGFELLOW,
from *The Song of Hiawatha*

RELIGION AND WAR

Each man's attitude toward his fellow man and the world about him has great significance in the quest for world political unity. His attitude towards others is in greatest measure shaped by his deepest philosophical motivation and, since this usually stems from his religious beliefs, it is essential that we treat here those factors in world religions that would reveal whether or not there exists a world-wide basic spiritual oneness in man's most serious efforts to come to grips with those fundamental problems of life that all men must face.

In its broadest sense, religion is a way of life concerned with the ultimate objectives of living. Extreme piety and searching metaphysical thought are often, but not necessarily, a part of religion. But there can be dangers in an excess of concern for the supernatural when unearthly things keep our attention from pressing earthly needs. When asked about the other world, Confucius would return his listener to this world and focus on man. He was urged to discuss serving the spirits of the dead. His reply: "While you are not able to serve man, how can you serve their spirits?" Confucius acknowledged supernatural power, but it did not consume his time. His philosophy was: one world at a time. The great lesson for modern man to be drawn from this thinking is that we must not use our religion as an escape mechanism whereby we lose ourselves in piousness and concern for the supernatural in a conscious or subconscious flight from the staggering problems of our modern world.

Darwin said that "a creed gives . . . the best practical hope that man can have for really controlling his future fate."[1] As our fate is common in the face of the universal threat to our very species, man must now so shape the ideals by which he lives that they reflect a concern for the fate of all men. Concern for state and nation must now be subordinated to concern for mankind. Brotherhood is today's practicality.

By reviewing the religions of the world, we find in each rewarding ideas that can be used to shape our thinking, ideas hundreds of years old that can serve us mightily as we seek a universal way to avoid universal calamity.

Taoism (pronounced dhowism) was founded over five hundred years before the birth of Christ. It is a Chinese religion whose classic work is the *Tao teh Ching*. From its pages come the following words:

"So far as arms are concerned, they are implements of ill omen. They are not implements for the man of Tao. For the actions of arms will be well requited: where armies are quartered brambles and thorns grow."

Tao means "road" or "way" and the *Tao teh Ching*, written by Taoism's founder Lao Tzu, means the way and its power. Also, from this book comes the following passage:

"One who would guide a leader
of men in the uses of life

1. Charles Galton Darwin, *The Next Million Years*, Garden City, Doubleday, 1953.

Will warn him against the use
of arms for conquest.
Even the finest arms are an
instrument of evil;
An army's harvest is a waste
of thorns.
In time of war men civilized in
peace
Turn from their higher to their
lower nature.
But triumph is not beautiful
He who thinks triumph beautiful
Is one with a will to kill.
The death of a multitude is
cause for mourning.
Conduct your triumph as a
funeral."

Also from this ancient book comes this admonition, "The way for a vital man to go is not the way of the soldier." And only the man "who recognizes all men as members of his own body is a sound man. . . . Heaven arms with compassion those whom she would not see destroyed."

More than four hundred years before the birth of Christ another great teacher, Confucius, saw moral law as forming one single system by which heaven and earth support and contain all things. He saw this oneness in everything that makes the universe so impressively great. In the writings of Confucius, we find these words similar to the Golden Rule: "What I would not have others to do to me, I do not do unto them" and "never do unto others what you would not like them to do to you."

As with Lao Tzu, the founder of Taoism, Confucius was chiefly concerned with things of this world. He had little to say of life beyond. Again, when asked about death he said, "Why ask me about death, when you do not know how to live?"

Confucius prescribed virtues which were much like those of Greek Stoicism. He thought of himself not as an innovator but rather as a transmitter of ancient truth. In his concept of the social strata, he thought the scholar was the highest, the soldier the lowest because he destroys what others produce. In fact, Confucius held a low estimate of the military generally.

He believed that all species have a basic instinct to join together in a reasonable peace. He felt this instinct is the cohesive force that holds the town, herd, drove and hive together, and that by recognizing and utilizing this instinct within a species, violence can be held to a minimum.

There was in existence during Confucius' time a philosophy known as Mohism, named after its principal spokesman, Mo Tzu or Mo Ti. It saw, as do many modern Christians, that social problems can be solved by love. Peace, it taught, lay in brotherly love: "feel kindly towards all people under heaven exactly as one feels toward one's own people, regard other States exactly as one regards one's own State." This was the Mohist injunction. Nearly five hundred years before Christ, Mo Tzu proclaimed this thesis: "Mutual attacks among states, mutual usurpation among houses, mutual injuries among individuals ... these are among the major calamities in the world.

"But where do these calamities arise? They arise out of want of mutual love."

But Confucius saw, as we must see today, that total reliance on love alone to solve all social problems is impractical. To expect that love will bring peace without the strictures of law and government was and is unrealistic; just government is the way a society expresses its concern and love of mankind.

We could well direct more of our social emphasis in America toward our families and, as Confucius, recognize that the family is the basic center of our society on which government must rely.

Finally, Confucius saw all men as brothers with a common bond between them. In Confucianism the term *Jen* involves a sense of dignity toward known life wherever it is. It knows no boundaries and states that "within the four seas all men are brothers."

Zoroastrianism has a most limited following. It is confined now chiefly to the Bombay area of India and to Iran. Founded by Zoroaster in Persia over six hundred years before the birth of Christ, it had its effect on the Jewish and Christian faiths because Persia ruled Palestine from 539-331 B.C. Particular emphasis was placed by Zoroaster on the equality and brotherhood of all men. The main theme of his teaching was the responsibility of man toward the universe in which he lives.

There was no founder of Hinduism; it simply evolved from antiquity. Krishna is the historic spokesman for this faith and the *Bhagavad Gita*, the most popular scripture, is found in the great epic of India, the *Mahabarata*.

While Krishna is seen as an incarnation of God, the Hindus believe such a wonder can repeat itself, and thus they would not necessarily deny the incarnation of God in Jesus, Rama, Buddha or other great spiritual figures and prophets.

Some writers have emphasized those Hindu sects that have become warlike, but Hinduism has its other side. There is conflicting evidence as to the attitude of Krishna

toward killing, but of great significance in any appraisal
of Hinduism is the fact that Gandhi found in it support
for his movement of non-violence. Gandhi was often
referred to as the most Christ-like man of his time. Yet,
he was not Christian, but drew his inspiration largely from
the *Bhagavad Gita* and from the philosophy and traditions
of his native India.

Our American writer-philosopher, Thoreau, said that
his mind was made by the *Bhagavad Gita* and Emerson's
Essay on Nature.

To the Hindu pleasure is not bad, but rather too trivial
to occupy his total time, too small in essence to claim
his perpetual enthusiasm. According to Hinduism, if we
follow an undeviating quest for pleasure, our reactions
become jaded and our satisfaction becomes ever more
elusive. Success, pleasure—although not evils—as our
chief concerns, cause us to search more and more for
enjoyments which become increasingly harder to find.

Hinduism suggests to the pleasure seeker that he
become less concerned with self and more involved with
the over-all human enterprise. Herein lies a great truth
the citizens of our own nation might take to heart; we
indulge ourselves with our own abundance while we remain seemingly oblivious to the need for international law
and government to serve the two thirds of humanity that
staggers under an overpowering burden of misery.

All great religions have been founded east of Suez;
four of them in India. One of these four is Buddhism.
The Buddha, born in 567 B.C., has been described as an
example of profound compassion for the welfare of others.

Buddhism prescribes social tolerance and inveighs
against stealing, lying, sexual immorality, killing and the
use of narcotics and intoxicants. It decrys wealth and
objects of desire and places emphasis on love. "Hatred

does not cease hatred at any time; hatred ceases by love. This is an old rule," said the Buddha. This is not unlike the passage in the Bible (Matthew 5:44) in which Jesus said, "I say unto you: Love your enemies, pray for those who persecute you." But Buddhists like Christians have, on occasion, permitted their nations to use them for human slaughter in war.

Whereas Jesus taught, "Thou shall not kill," Buddha went further, prohibiting the killing of even sub-human life. He directed his followers to shun forever violence and force as methods of spreading the doctrine, and it is felt that Buddhism has a firmer pacifist basis than Christianity. While this may be true, Buddha and Jesus were on the whole as one in their ethical thinking. This is particularly true on the matters of war and peace. And while Buddhism is non-theistic, it, with Christianity, agrees that there is a moral order in the universe that supports good and condemns evil.

Buddha felt that the butcher, brewer, tax collector and armament maker held roles that were incompatible with spiritual advancement. He sought a wider understanding among all people in the belief that by knowing one another we are relieved of our fear which is generally learned out of ignorance. He believed that by knowing and understanding others we will become interested in their problems and gain respect for them as human beings. Buddha would have therefore agreed with Spinoza that, "To understand something is to be delivered of it."

The influence of Buddhism is spreading today. It now has over 350 million followers in nine nations and thousands of Buddhists have become citizens of the United States with the admission of Hawaii to the Union.

A contemporary of the Buddha was Mahavira, who went far beyond Jesus in the matter of not taking life. To be saved we must practice *ahimsa*, i.e., non-injury and non-killing even of subhuman life.

The Jains are required to take five vows not to harm any living creature. Some few Jains have entered military service, but as with Christians, Buddhists, and Taoists such action cannot be justified by anything its founder taught or practiced.

The philosophy of Mahavira is reflected in one of his sayings, "In happiness and suffering, in joy and grief, we should regard all creatures as we regard our own self, and should refrain from afflicting upon others such injury as would appear undesirable to us if inflicted upon ourselves."

Nanak was the latest born of the great religious founders. He was a contemporary of Martin Luther, having been born in 1470. Nanak founded the religion of the Sikhs.

Sikhs are often associated with Hinduism, but Sikhs themselves disavow and disclaim any connection. In reality this religion is the result of the fusion of some of the aspects of the Hindu and Moslem faiths.

Nanak paid no heed to the rigid caste system that separated his people, but he went among every class and welcomed all people as his followers.

He taught that while God is supreme truth, omnipresent and universal, he is also a personal God.

Christians, it is feared, often tend to see God more as apart from nature and man, controlling them, caring for them, effecting his purpose among and through them. Nanak saw God as having these powers and at the same time as being one of the people. This personal identification with God, the lack of remoteness of God in the Sihk belief, commends itself to the Christian.

There is a strong tendency now to amalgamate Sikhism and the Hindu faith. Even if Sikhism eventually loses its separate identity it has played a significant role in the outlawing of the caste system in modern India.

At the height of their influence the Muslims had an empire that reached from the Atlantic to China, an empire bigger than the Roman Empire at its zenith.

Allah was but one of the Gods being worshipped in Mecca during Mohammed's stay there, but he began to see Allah as the only God. Mohammed, according to Islamic belief, was given the power by this all-powerful deity to write the scripture of Islam, the *Koran*. It is the most read, most memorized and most influential book in the world. The *Koran* is said to be grammatically perfect and without poetic equal.

A Muslim would readily agree that Christ was one of the world's great prophets, but would argue that in claiming Him to be the incarnation of God, we Christians compromise the monotheistic quality of Christianity. Muslims would interpret Christ's statement that he was the Son of God as an affirmation that all men are God's children and with this all Muslims would agree. They see man as creature not creator, Mohammed and Christ as prophets not deities.

Islam stresses that every corner of God's universe is equally pure and that there is absolute equality among the races. To stress this point, Mohammed himself intermarried.

In some areas in which Christianity and Islam are competing for adherents and especially in Africa, Islam is gaining converts at a rate of 10 to 1 over Christianity. It may well be the fastest growing religion in the world and presently has some 400,000,000 followers.

The greeting used by Muslims throughout the world is "salam" which means "peace." And while Muslims have at times resorted to military conquest as have the followers of other religions, the *Koran* directs each follower of Islam to "Defend yourself against your enemies; but attack them not first; God hateth the aggressor."

The Ten Commandments of Hebraic morality, which have been adopted by Christianity and Islam, make up the moral foundation of one half the present world population. It is Jewish doctrine that all men are members of a single family. According to Jewish legend, when God made Adam of clay he gathered it from every corner of the earth and of every clan to insure the basic homogeneity of man.

Moses received the Jewish *Torah*, which comprises the first five books of the Christian Bible, directly from the hand of God. The word *Torah* means "law" and according to Jewish belief Moses, after receiving the law from God, descended from the mountain and told his people of Yahweh (God) and the law.

From the beginning, Jewish doctrine has been to establish goodness not only among themselves but everywhere and to teach that the moral law is both eternal and universal.

The nation of Israel owes its existence in large measure to the United Nations. Thus, this relatively new country has from its creation had a close touch with universal political action.

From the standpoint of both her ancient traditions and modern history, the state of Israel will find no insuperable problems as it one day joins with other nations in a strengthened universal political alliance for peace. Jews everywhere will find both in their heart and in their faith a welcome for the coming of a world under just law.

It is impossible to separate today's Shintoism historically from Chinese and Buddhist influences. Taoism and the Yin-Yang philosophy have also had great effect in shaping Shintoism, the religious cult indigenous to the Japanese Islands. This faith has been referred to as an amalgamation of Japanese tradition, Buddhism, Confucianism and Taoism.

Shintoism presents an excellent modern illustration of a faith that has been used in times of national crises to justify killing and self-destruction. The word *Kami* describes anything holy. *Kamikaze* means "devine wind" and refers to the storm that destroyed the Chinese invasion fleet of Kublai Khan off the coast of Japan in the 13th Century.

Extreme militarists and nationalists during World War II convinced large numbers of Japanese soldiers, sailors and pilots that by suicide action directed at the enemy they could demonstrate their loyalty to the emperor and to the motherland. According to the jingoistic preachments of that time, one dying bravely in battle became an illustrious ancestor, joining the *Kami* beings of the spirit world, thereby surviving death and securing to himself everlasting life.

The Japanese people, as much as any people on earth, now know the horrors of war and have resolved to find practical approaches to peace. They have unmasked the militarists that would twist Shintoism into an aggressive war-faith for narrow militaristic purposes. Japan now stands ready to join with other nations of the world in establishing an international political framework of law and government to prevent any future tragedies such as were suffered in the nuclear bombings of Nagasaki and Hiroshima.

The Christian in the Search for Peace

The religious book of Christ's youth was the sacred Jewish *Torah*. But Jesus was a prophet critical of his heritage. He could rightly be called a "subversive" of his day. He clearly felt that there was more truth to be known and revealed. It was rank heresy for Him to say: "You have heard it of old time . . . but I say unto you. . . ." To the Romans He was clearly a dangerous revolutionary. But He believed in law and its enrichment: "I came not to destroy the law. . . ." He made clear that there are things that outweigh in importance the national state that must command man's first allegiance when he said, "Render unto Caesar those things that are Caesar's and unto God the things that are God's."

Christianity is the most wide-spread religion in the world today and has the largest number of adherents. Nearly one out of every four people in the world—some 895 million—claim the Christian faith, but what of the other 75 per cent of the world's population?

While Christianity is the largest single religion it by no means is a majority religion. It is interesting to note the number of adherents claimed by each of the major religions:

Buddhism—350,000,000	Judaism—12,000,000
Christianity—895,000,000	Shintoism—25,000,000
Confucianism—300,000,000	Sikhism—6,250,000
Hinduism—300,000,000	Taoism—50,000,000
Islam—400,000,000	Zoroastrianism—1,000,000
Jainism—1,500,000	

Since it has been noted that Islam in some areas is growing at a greater rate than is Christianity, Christians might well become concerned lest the universal influence of their faith begins to wane. This concern is made more poignant in the light of the prediction that the world's population will double by 2000 A.D.

The Baha'i church represents the modern syncretistic faith, but a synthesis of religions is not necessary to an understanding and respect for the universality of basic principles that undergird man's searchings for the way to ultimate truth. In a politically universal world there need be no single spiritual tradition. Yet in matching and hopefully exceeding scientific achievements with advancements in human relations, we best have a basic understanding of other approaches to the universal problems of living. This will bring to us a respect for those of foreign tongues and lands. With such respect there will follow a lessening of fear and prejudice and a Christian church more closely in harmony with the life and teachings of Jesus.

In referring to the problems of race relations facing the South, Bishop William T. Watkins of the Methodist Church said, "As ministers, we make ourselves ludicrous if we proclaim the fatherhood of God and leave off the brotherhood of man."[2] Ministers should be ever aware that "He hath made of one blood all nations for to dwell on the face of the earth."

Intolerance is hard to combat even in the pulpit. It is easy to speak against "godless communism" but fail to take note of the far greater evils practiced in some non-communist countries, i.e., Spain and Saudi Arabia. Ministers should be ever aware, too, that while a nation may begin with the premise that there is God, "If a man say, I love God, and hateth his brother, he is a liar; for he that loveth not his brother whom he has seen, how can he love God whom he hath not seen?"[3] Thus, the fact that a nation is

2. From an article by Bishop William T. Watkins, *World Outlook*, August, 1960.

3. John 4:20-16.

tolerant of religion does not insure that the government will act in a Christian manner toward its citizens. Conversely, where religion is not encouraged by the national government this does not mean per se that the citizens are enslaved or treated unjustly.

Over 81,000 Jehovah's Witnesses from sixty-seven nations meeting in Yankee Stadium on August 4, 1950, unanimously declared: "Extreme pacifism is not our preachment. We are not pacifists. We fight with the sword of the spirit, the Bible. We come from a long line of fighters . . . running all the way back to Abel and including Moses, Joshua, Barak, Jephahah, Gideon, Samson, and David, all warriors from Jehovah. Christ Jesus is our Commander and is Jehovah's greatest fighter in the universe. We follow in His footsetps by preaching and fighting for the Theocracy, but not in violent ways."

There is underlying truth in this statement in that there is no contradiction in opposing war while at the same time fighting for peace with justice under law and government. There is inconsistency in claiming to be Christian and not fighting for an international political and social posture that will allow international anarchy to be replaced by law and order.

Since the Reformation, there have been a number of pacifist churches—the Minnonites, Hutterites, Socinians, Quakers and Brethren—among others. Surely these groups have been fighters for peace while opposing war; the work of the American Friends Service Committee being the outstanding example of Christian faith in action. No one contends that pacifism must become universal or even widespread before peace can be realized. There must be a realization on the part of the non-pacifist that international warfare is opposed to the best interests of his nation; that his traditional concept of patriotism as a

willingness to die for his country should be re-examined;
that law and government, not H-bombs and nerve gas,
hold the greatest hope for his nation. Men must become
witnesses for this concept of patriotism. It is not cowardly
to stand up for one's country. It may be more difficult to
stand for progress through world government and law
than to be actively engaged in the military forces, but we
are now in an age in which the destiny of each nation is
inextricably intertwined with that of the other nations of
the world. International war has now become the antithesis of patriotism as has each of those multitudinous
pressures brought to bear on the individual citizen to keep
him a part of the traditional military-patriotism philosophy.

No minister should ever be guilty of invoking Christ
to justify nuclear annihilation. Preachers that condemn a
nation, a people or a form of government without pin-
pointing the evil to which they object in specific terms,
aside from being guilty of poor preparation and scholar-
ship, add to the hysteria that sets the people of one nation
against the people of other areas of the world. Ministers
should inveigh against specific evils and suggest specific
cures. Great harm and no good comes from building blind
hatred against that nation or people currently on the
"outs" with their own nation. Informed criticism of
injustices both at home and abroad is clearly one of the
most constructive functions of the Christian ministry. But
it should be clear that homilies, generalities and hatreds
will not cure the ills of the world or bring dignity and
justice to its people. The time has come when ministers
should either stand for universal brotherhood or sit down.

The minister should remember that what he seeks is
not just an idyllic peace in which "the wolf shall dwell

with the lamb."[4] but that he also seeks something less idyllic and far more necessary, a world in which we rise to a new plateau in man's relationship with man, a world in which the brotherhood of man can have a chance to flourish in an atmosphere conducive to reason; a world in which the moral conscience of man can be brought to bear on man's inhumanity to man within an international framework of justice under law. Is there a Christian minister who is not supremely troubled when he sees a clean-cut young man from his congregation drafted into the armed forces and taught every conceivable method of killing other young men just like himself whose only crime is that they are not American?

There appeared one day in a Southern newspaper a letter from a lady that listed six requisites for world peace; they were:

1. Read the Bible prayerfully each day;
2. When entering the House of God give thanks and praise;
3. Pray daily;
4. Obey God's will at all times;
5. Spread the Gospel;
6. Train more old fashion Holiness preachers, who can preach a sermon instead of reading one.

This exemplifies one of the dangers ministers must avoid. Extreme piety and a lack of concern for specifics will surely not bring world peace. "Faith without works is dead" is a much quoted Biblical phrase, but it never had more pertinent application than to the role of the Christian in the search for peace.

At a world affairs conference after many experts on international problems had spoken on the need for in-

4. Isaiah 11:6-9.

dividuals to address themselves to the threat of war that hangs over all mankind, a small lady slowly rose from her seat and said: "World peace will come when all men turn to Christ."

The difficulty with paths to peace outlined by the letterwriter and the conferee is that they show concern for the form of religion—prayer, preachments, proselyting—without regard for religious substance, i.e., how do we correct inequities, feed the hungry, cloth the naked and secure peace with justice under law? Religious form can be used as a shield with which to defend oneself against the spiritual and physical facts of life; such a philosophy can be a cozy, sanctimonious refuge within which the believer can find peace of mind and secure from his associates a reputation for being a "good" man.

To avoid such religious sterility, ministers should inform themselves about the United Nations, national and international problems and avail themselves of the opportunity to attend and participate in world affairs conferences. They should speak out on such issues as the need for world government, the sharing of surplus food; encourage their parishioners to visit foreign lands, in particular the "out" nations to gain first-hand information; they should become informed as to the best ways to convert the national economy from a war to a peace time footing, counseling that any privations involved should be suffered in good will as one of the prices of world peace. Ministers should advocate the giving to the United Nations and to peace organizations of an amount of money commensurate with that which we give to the government for the preparation of war; and, possibly most importantly, they should speak out to the effect that the sovereignty of man surpasses in importance the sovereignty of any nation. The Bible lays emphasis on activity when it says

not blessed are the peaceable, but "blessed are the peace-
makers." There is a positive Christian duty to be informed and active in peace efforts.

A minister's congregation should have no doubt but
that he places service to God above service to country;
that, since there is some of the Divine in each of us, service
to mankind is service to God. He should always strive
to have his congregation numbered among those whose
first concern is allegiance to God through man. The effect
of the ministers' counsel should be to heal bodies, not to
destroy them; to cast out fear, not to generate it; to seek
understanding, not damnation. In no small degree a nation
reaps what its ministers sow. Great care should be
used in the sowing as we do not gather "grapes of thorns
or figs of thistles." As war transgresses every command-
ment in the Decalogue and repudiates the Sermon on the
Mount, the true man of God will seek constructively to
prevent international war, this desecration of God's handiwork.

There will arise on occasion those who will advocate
a "holy war" as the path to peace. Ironically the Christian
religion has been invoked to justify some of man's grim-
mest rampages into torture and injustice. The army of
Oliver Cromwell was stimulated with prayerful exhorta-
tions by their leader who was a dedicated Christian, but
the persecutions levied by this army on the Roman
Catholics of Ireland compare with the savagery of any
army of recorded history.

The Inquisition in Europe had its beginnings in the
fourth century, developed in the intervening centuries and
reached its fullest development from the thirteenth to the
eighteenth centuries. During this period, the Church had
men tried for crimes of heresy, apostasy, witchcraft,
necromancy, bigamy, blasphemy and usury. Torture was

recognized by the Church as an accepted means of gaining evidence. No one accused was permitted counsel or witnesses; torture chambers were freely employed. No one charged received a complete acquittal, and punishment ran from damnation to death; property confiscation was common and torture was widespread. When a sentence was death, it would be administered by strangulation or fire.

The Children's Crusade of 1212 A.D. sent some 30,000 French children and 20,000 Italian children to death, slavery, prostitution and torture; but the Crusades were begun by dedicated militant Christians who were convinced that it was God's will that they wrest the Holy Land from the Mohammedans.

Thousands of Protestants in France were killed in repetitions of the Massacre of St. Bartholomew in 1572. These killings were instigated by Catherine de Medici, Queen of France, and for her actions she received the congratulations of Pope Gregory XIII who thereupon had a medal struck in her honor.

And so it goes. We must be ever alert in our time to those who would under the guise of carrying out God's will seek to foment hatred and sow the seeds of war and murder in the name of Christianity.

In conspicuous contrast is the Papal Encyclical *Pacem In Terris* (Peace on Earth) of Pope John XXIII on April 10, 1963. This letter, instead of being addressed just to Catholics, was issued to "all men of good will" and proposed a supranational world political order for "problems of worldwide dimensions." The letter stated that justice for humanity demands that the arms race cease; that nuclear weapons be banned and that general agreement should eventually be reached on progressive disarmament and effective methods of arms control, and that every trace of racism should be eliminated. The Pope called on states to recognize their duty to aid all political refugees and to protect essential personal rights of each and every individual.

A portion of the encyclical dealing with world authority reads as follows: "Today the universal common good poses problems of worldwide dimensions, which cannot be adequately tackled or solved except by efforts of public authorities endowed with a wideness of powers, structure and means of the same proportions; that is, of public authorities which are in a position to operate in an effective manner on a worldwide basis. The moral order itself, therefore, demands that such a form of public authority be established." It was this call for world authority to deal with world problems that was the key to the Pontiff's highly important encyclical termed by some as the Magna Carta of the Catholic Church. Church leaders both Catholic and non-Catholic today see more clearly how imperative is the attainment of universal political unity as a Christian duty.

But many of those who have never known war get their impressions of war from those whose memories have been dulled by the passing years. It is a human characteristic to forget the terrors, savagery and loneliness of war and remember the exciting releases it affords. To one man it may have broken a boring office routine; to another freedom from an oppressive domestic situation. Some men's memories linger on debauchery—the wine they drank, the women they knew. To thousands it was in fact a vacation of sorts; a release from their humdrum existence; a welcomed relief.

But there are other thousands. Some of these men lie here in American and in twenty-two cemeteries abroad. One such cemetery is at Saint-Laurent-sur-Mer in France near what was known as Omaha Beach during World War

II; 9,386 Americans are buried there. White crosses and stars of David stretch in endless array into the distance to become blended and lost to the eye in the mist of the English Channel. A father and son lie together; thirty pairs of brothers lie side by side. The names of 1,556 Americans are inscribed on a wall in the Garden of the Missing under the words: "This is their memorial, the whole earth their sepulchre."

The sight and silence impress the viewer with awe and a welling sadness that so many died so young in a conflict that was—while refined and more savage—essentially no different from that of the raiding tribes of antiquity.

A staggering total of 407,316 American servicemen died in World War II. Esitmates of the number of Americans that would die in the first few stages of a nuclear war range from 10 to 160 million. It would be well for every Christian minister each year to visit one of the cemeteries where our young war dead lie and to reflect on the gross tragedy of their death; most of all to contemplate the fact that they died at the hands of other young men who, as the dead, had been sent out to kill and be killed in a process devoid of law, reason or morality.

One of the men buried at Omaha Beach was from Georgia and a member of the 501st Parachute Infantry Regiment. He spent the day before he died at a temporary airfield called Merryfield in England absorbing information about an area of France designated as Drop Zone D. Late in the afternoon, loaded down with military equipment, his regiment was marched out to be flown across the English Channel to be dropped into combat. As they marched someone in the ranks began to sing a song set to the tune of "The Battle Hymn of the Republic."

"Glory, glory, what a hell of a way to die,
Glory, glory, what a hell of a way to die,
Glory, glory, what a hell of a way to die,
And we won't have to jump no more."

Now this young boy from Georgia lies buried near a twenty-foot bronze statue of a young man his arms reaching toward the sky. The statue is called "The Spirit of American Youth."

Obviously, those who plan and who are guilty of international crimes should be punished. The trials at Nuremberg and Tokyo resulted in the punishment of some war criminals, but others escaped imprisonment and were assimilated into succeeding economies and governments to lend their warped talents to another cycle of armament production and war preparation.

One such war planner is General Miroru Genda, retired chief of the Japanese Air Force. General Genda, who helped plan the attack on Pearl Harbor in 1941, was awarded the Legion of Merit by the United States in 1961. This is the highest award our country bestows upon a foreigner and it was pinned on General Genda by the chairman of the U. S. Joint Chiefs of Staff, General Lyman L. Lemnitzer. The reason given for decorating General Genda was that he had been instrumental in building up Japan's air forces since the 1951 Peace Treaty.

But what of the young men that were killed in the international warfare planned by the General Gendas? Are the boys who lie under crosses around the world to be remembered only on Veterans Day and then only by the few?

It is a concern for those who have died and for those who live in peril of being offered as sacrifices to the idol of the nation-state that should move every man of the cloth to devote a large portion of his time to the creation of an ordered world of just law and government wherein the youth of the world are allowed to live out their lives in freedom under enforceable world law. They should seek a world rule of law wherein international criminals are held accountable in courts of law for their actions and wherein nations do not waste themselves and their property in periodic and senseless combat.

Even the greatest of men can fall victim to savagery if it is the custom of the day. No visitor to the magnificent home of Thomas Jefferson at Monticello, Virginia, can come away without being confused by the fact that this great champion of human rights owned slaves. In unabashed frankness tourists visiting this national shrine are shown through Jefferson's extensive slave quarters.

While some three million slaves were shipped across the Atlantic in the seventeenth century, it is estimated that in the century of the birth of the United States seven million Africans were taken from their homes for shipment to the New World. From 1518 to 1865, fifteen million slaves were delivered in this traffic in human lives. It was an open question among slavers of this era whether to "tight pack" their cargo or permit them enough room to lie on their backs. The "loose packers" argued that more slaves would survive in the ship's hold if they could lie back. The "tight packers" held to the theory that only enough room should be permitted for slaves to lie on their sides. While more died by the "tight pack" method the over-all number of live deliveries was greater.

The brutality aboard these ships knew no limit. Captain Homans of the British brig *Brillante* tied 600 slaves to his anchor chain and threw them overboard to avoid being caught with the evidence of his guilt after England outlawed the slave trade in 1807. While England was the first of the slave-trading Western powers to try to suppress the business of trading in human life, it continued on the high seas for at least another half-century.

How could men like Jefferson own slaves? When pressed for an explanation, slave owners would repair to the sanctuary of the Old Testament and recite Leviticus 25:44—"Thy bondmen shall be of the heathen."

There are areas in which a clergyman must distinguish himself from the customs of his day, take his stand with eternal truths and not seek sanction for barbarism in his Bible. The quintessence of theological perversion is the use of the Bible to justify inhumanity. There is no clearer, no more damnable violation of this principle than when a minister employs the Old Testament to either justify international warfare or to avoid taking a position in opposition to international warfare.

Conclusions

People differ everywhere in superficial ways, but there is an overriding human belief in a transcendent moral law which should guide man in his relationship with his fellowman. This world-wide inherent understanding does not stop at the borders of Communist nations as any world traveler can testify. Within our world-wide community there are differences of approach, but agreement on fundamental human rights and basic truths understood by the peoples of all nations.

Each of the great religions is a blend of universal principles and local traditions. When emphasis is placed on the variations in custom and ritual, religions can be made to appear completely different. But the essence of each religion is its striving to see more clearly the infinite reality of truth with the finite vision of man. Since a complete revelation of ultimate reality can never be fully grasped by the finite mind of man, how can he say positively that any single religion bears the complete truth? Arnold Toynbee feels that, "There is no one alive today who knows enough to say with confidence whether our religion has been greater than all others." Individuals then who would seek true knowledge of the world and its people and who would be effective in working to promote an international political order, should place their emphasis on comparative religion rather than competitive religion, trying to discover the points of similarity and universal binding qualities among all the great faiths.

We in the United States are steeped in the Greek, Roman and Judeo-Christian traditions. However, more than any single nation it is from India that man has received directions and writings dealing with the perfection of the inner life. Students of anthropology tell us that no society of man has ever been found that did not have some form of religious expression. Virtually all societies—both theistic and atheistic—have the equivalent of the Ten Commandments to check the savagery in man and to make it possible for him to develop his culture and civilization. The conspicuous exception is at the world level of man's society where initial steps have been taken to control the armaments of nations, but the journey is far from completed.

Freud believed that religion is the expression of neuroses based on guilt inherent in the repression of infantile sexual fantasies. More appealing and probable is the view that religion is man's recognition of his own need to be associated more closely with the unknown forces in the order of the universe before which he stands in awe. Religion serves as man's bridge to ultimate truth and salvation, his effort to span the chasm of the unknown.

The Latin word *salutas* means safety. In this sense "salvation" is common to all religions and, in fact, is their primary concern. Each religion seeks to present a meaningful formula for an harmonious existence within the cosmos, and regardless of what is believed to be one's destiny after death, to present a method of steeling the follower to face the terrifying factors of hopelessness, sickness, and death.

To enhance the claimed authority of a particular faith, myth and legend in time become engrafted. In as much as religion is the means of discovering the virtuous way and since ultimate truth is involved with the very substance of reality, then a religion traditionally must have some tie with the supernatural. Those who have recorded religious teaching have tended to embellish their writings with miracles to fill this seemingly compelling need to identify with the supernatural. Often it has been done by ascribing to a founder of religion miraculous experiences which are designed to leave the impression that God has directly bestowed on the discoverer of the faith unique insight and unearthly transcendant powers. And because religious writings and teachings are subject to various interpretations, there is little doubt that today's teachings of some religions would startle and possibly even outrage the original authors.

The early development of religion was characterized by ascribing life and super-human qualities to natural phenomena—the sun, moon, wind, sea, sky, stars, mountains, and rivers. As religious thought developed, man tended to see infinite wisdom in human form or at least revealed through man.

Because truth is infinite, we can search but never fully understand it, and since it is common in some measure to all men, it would seem to follow that we may find some of its revelations in religions other than our own. At the very least, we should respect the genuine strivings of others to see more clearly the ultimate reality of the cosmic order.

Normally, a man will seek ultimate reality and truth through the medium most commonly used in his own culture. A non-Jewish citizen of the United States would tend to become a Christian and to belong to the denomination of his parents. This point can even be extended to the atheistic belief of communism. A youth born in a communist nation would tend to gravitate to the view that communism held the key to the most rewarding existence for himself and his society.

Danger lies for us in feeling that our own culture and beliefs are exclusively or completely good. If ultimate truth and reality are universal, it cannot be the province of one nation or one people alone. If ultimate truth is omnipotent and omnipresent, it reveals itself in various ways through differing devices and different peoples. As each man seeks to climb the mountain to the summit of supreme awareness, he increasingly tends to feel that the path he has chosen is the best, even the only path. He then tries to convert others to follow the path he has chosen and in so doing, he may become intolerant and disruptive of those who are climbing the same mountain by an equally direct but different way. We should remember that at the summit all pathways merge.

Seeking to understand and respect those of other beliefs will enrich our lives and promote international understanding which is so much to be desired as we approach the creation of a world government.

While ultimate truth is universal, the efforts to seek out this truth need not be. Water is the same by whatever name it may be called in various parts of the world. It may be called *eau, agua, pani,* etc. Similarly, God and truth are universal, but he may be called Allah, Jehovah, Brahman, etc.

Finally, and by way of summary, the basic point is that there is a tremendous variety of approaches to the universal principles by which man can find worthiness in his existence and so direct his life that it will be meaningfully rewarding for himself and his fellow man. Within the United States, there are literally hundreds of denominations of the Christian religion each reflecting in some degree a divergence of approach to the reality that all men seek. Regardless of the pathway we choose, we will be individually better and our lives of greater moment if we respect, and learn from, the pathways to the ultimate summit chosen by other peoples. Most important that we resist attempts to use our religion or the religion of others to generate animosities or to justify violence among men. Conversely, there is the positive duty resting on each of us to combine his faith with work in behalf of the great enterprise of bringing national armies under the control of law and government.

". . . Where nature makes natural allies of us all we can demonstrate that beneficial relations are possible even with those with whom we most deeply disagree—and this must some day be the basis of world peace and world law."

State of the Union Message
January, 1961

". . . We seek to strengthen the United Nations, to help solve its financial problems, to make it a more effective instrument for peace, to develop it into a genuine world security system . . . capable of resolving disputes on the basis of law, of insuring the security of the large and the small, and of creating conditions under which arms can finally be abolished. . . . This will require a new effort to achieve world law. . . ."

American University Speech
June, 1963

"Your consistent support of the United Nations and your unflagging advocacy of the means whereby it might be strengthened represent a genuine contribution to public education. As you foresaw at the founding of your organization in 1947, world law still remains the world's best choice for avoiding world war."

Message to United World
Federalists, May, 1963

—JOHN F. KENNEDY

PART

III | # WORLD LAW AND THE FORCE OF HISTORY

World Law
International Court of Justice
The Future of the United Nations

WORLD LAW

The word "law" may be used in several ways; for example, it may be used to describe the scientific phenomenon that controls the order of the universe. The word "law" may also be used to explain certain group tendencies found by the social sciences. But within the field of jurisprudence the word is used chiefly to denote rules prescribed for human action by man himself, enforceable in courts of justice.

Law in this latter sense had its derivation in man's concept of what ought to be done; it has the quality of normalcy generally reflecting the norms of the society. One who fails to obey these norms generally must suffer penalty. In order to insure compliance with law as a prescription for human conduct, the society through history has imposed various pressures on the individual to comply with the law; these have included fines, imprisonment, mutilation, whipping, exile and death.

Law has historically required official or quasi-official enforcement on behalf of the society whether it be imposed by the family head, the tribal chief or a more imposing government. Historically, too, a violation of the law or social norm has been an act against the society as a whole, with punishment, in more recent history,

coming from the injured society with the private prosecutor, the public prosecutor, the policeman and the judge
acting in society's behalf to apply the law and redress the
injured social conscience.

Law in the sense of prescribed human action must:

(a) be a social norm;
(b) have the element of official authority behind it;
(c) be enforced by the application of sanctions prescribed by the society.

These elements are basic to prescribed law in virtually
every society.

Homicide is recognized as illegal and punishable
universally and at all strata of man's society. While what
constitutes homicide has certainly varied, it is nonetheless
true that certain types of human killing have always been
recognized as wrong and subject to legal control regardless of how primitive this control might be.

It is here that we find a rule of social conduct that is
not alone prescribed by the society but a norm inherent in
man. This aversion to taking the life of another is a
part of being human. This is not to say that man does not
kill; it is to say that he rationalizes his killing and that in
his reflective, quiet and pensive times when he is creative
and good he knows in his inner self that he should not kill.
To kill another human being is generally to violate a
universal social norm and a recognized moral law. It is
the insiduous activity of nation-states in converting natural
resources into materials of mass destruction and in co-
ercing their citizens to kill in war that constitutes the
striking need for world law through which the inherent
conscience of man can be brought to bear on the problem
of war.

The ages have brought about a constant shifting of the redress and prevention of illegal killing to higher and higher levels of government. Society as a whole having been injured, it has rightly fallen the lot of all people acting through their governments to enact law and impose sanctions to prevent war and to seek redress for those injured by war. Where justice could not be secured by government, because it lacked sufficient representation or power to act for the society, then redress was sought by means of self-help. This extra-judicial means of seeking justice has historically led to more conflict thereby promoting, not diminishing, warfare.

Legal means to prevent physical conflict have been found in every culture from primitive tribes to highly developed nation states. Similarly, means of punishing those who commit acts against the society have been devised and employed at various levels. As a result of the Nuremburg, Tokyo and Eichmann trials international criminal law is beginning to emerge to deal, after the fact, with those who violate international social norms in a criminal manner.[1]

It is difficult to improve on Cicero's definition of true law when he wrote, "There is, in fact, a true law, right reason in accordance with nature; it applies to all men and is eternal. It summons men to the performance of their duties, it restrains them from doing wrong. . . . to invalidate this law by human legislation is never morally right, nor is it permissible ever to restrict its operation, and to annul it wholly is impossible. Neither the senate nor the people can absolve us from our obligation to obey this law . . . binding at all times upon all peoples. . . . The man who will not obey it will abandon his better self, and, in denying the true nature of man, will thereby suffer

1. See Appendix B.

the severest of penalties though he has escaped all other consequences which men call punishments."

These truths are no less valid today than in the time of Cicero. However, some of the physical proportions of the world have now been changed or combined so as to make necessary the bringing to bear on the problem of war the full force of not only moral but juridical and governmental authority. It is now inimical to the best interests of the world community for a nation or military alliance of nations to have weapons of mass destruction entrusted to their arbitrary will. Through the ages runs the basic truth expressed by Cicero, and restated in many ways by countless scholars and teachers. Now national armies and armaments must be brought under the control of international law in the name of the world's peoples.

As Dean Henry P. Brandis, Jr., Dean of the University of North Carolina School of Law, has said, "We are not striving merely for peace—merely the absence of war, which would be gained by yielding to Communist aggression. The real desire and hope of all Americans is peace with freedom and justice, possible only under some form of effective world law to prevent aggression and preserve the internal sovereignty and freedom of the nations."[2]

President Kennedy, writing on our national purpose, wrote, ". . . we as a nation should drive for the attainment of world peace and disarmament, based on world law and order, on the mutual respect of free peoples, and on the world economy in which there are no 'have not' or 'underdeveloped' nations."[3]

Addressing his remarks to the theme "Is There Not a Cause?" J. W. Talley, Jr., President of Kiwanis Inter-

2. From an address given at the Fourth Annual Conference on World Affairs, February, 1954.

3. *Life*, August 22, 1960.

national, said, "I tell you there is such a cause, and I tell you what it is. It is the cause of the establishment of the rule of law in international affairs instead of the misrule and anarchy of clashing national governments. It is the cause of a working concern for the health, education and decency of all men everywhere. It is the cause of the active waging of peace.

"We need to march and work in this great cause. The evils and dangers of our world today are caused not just by Communists. We, too, are to blame. They are caused by our lack of high purpose and unselfish concern for the structure of our world and the people of our world.

"It can be the peoples of our land, already knowing freedom, who can lead our land and the rest of the world to the establishment of that freedom for all men under law and responsibility to international self-government, that, in Mr. Lincoln's words, 'not only this nation, but this world . . . under God, shall have a 'new birth of freedom.' "[4]

The International Court of Justice recognizes five sources of law, i.e., treaties, judicial decrees, the general principles of law recognized by civilized nations, customs, and the teachings of highly qualified scholars, the latter two being auxiliary and supplemental to the first three. Of great significance is the fact that a large number of the lawyers attending the First World Conference of Lawyers on World Peace Through Law held in Athens, Greece, in the summer of 1963, unofficially expressed the view that because of its practically universal acceptance the Declaration of Human Rights[5] has now the status of world law. It has become in the eyes of many—particularly those citizens of formerly oppressed nations who

4. Speaking in Toronto, Canada, August 26, 1960.
5. See Appendix A, this volume.

have recently gained their freedom—an international Bill of Rights. In view of the limited acceptance of the more formal Covenant of Human Rights the rising force of the Declaration of Human Rights should be welcomed by freedom-loving people everywhere.

Writing in the Journal of the American Bar Association, Benjamin H. Kizer expressed the view that those who trumpet their distrust for the World Court must bear a heavy responsibility for the want of progress in substituting world law for world anarchy and world tension. He wrote, "Throughout the history of mankind, the establishment of the rule of law has been the one great instrument that has assured domestic tranquility, that has substituted the courtroom for the duel and for the private vendetta; the principle of equality before the law in place of the rule of the strong and unscrupulous over the weak."[6]

What is the law to be applied among nations? Aside from the existing precedents in international custom and treaty law, the area of future international legal concern can be found in the present United Nations Charter and the Universal Declaration of Human Rights. Herein we find legal precepts that have been agreed to by the vast majority of the peoples of the earth.[7] It is for the World Court to take cognizance of matters that promote the purposes and rights expressed in these documents. In turn, it is for the General Assembly and the Security Council to take affirmative steps to see that the universal rights of man and the peace of the world are secured. In addition, the individual nations of the world must not hesitate to encourage the use of the good offices of the

6. *American Bar Association Journal*, Vol. 46, p. 930.

7. See Appendix A of this volume; see also Appendix B re Code of Offenses Against the Peace and Security of Mankind.

United Nations and the World Court and to bring to the Court for its adjudication matters of international moment.

In an expanded United Nations empowered to enact world law, the foundations of this law will be found, again, in the general principles of justice set forth in the Charter and the Declaration. The attainment of a consensus of general principles has been reached in the adoption of these documents by a large majority of the nations of the earth and this majority has steadily increased since the birth of the United Nations in 1945. We should not, therefore, be frightened by our unfamiliarity with world legal systems other than our own. A leading Scottish judge and jurist writing on the basis of his experience in the application of diverse legal systems from all areas of the world said, "No one can address himself to the study of comparative law without being struck by the essential similarity of the problem of human relationship all over the world, and despite the diversity in form of the solutions which each national system of law has devised, with the general resemblance in outline of their solutions."[8]

The fact is that those parts of the law which differ most widely as between various systems of law are the least important to the development of the future international legal system. These basic differences, although sometimes difficult to reconcile, are generally confined to ritual and matters of insubstantial moment to the development of peace-law. There is a great difference between the legal rituals of Hindu, Islamic and Jewish law. There are the complexities of the Hindu joint family system or the differences of the Sunnite and Shitite laws of inheritance. But Western influence on legal systems has been profound, as a matter of fact, it is only in Saudi Arabia and Yeman that Islamic law has survived without sub-

8. *The Law and Other Things*, Macmillan, 1939, p. 114.

stantial Western influence. In Turkey, the Islamic and Ottoman law has been considerably modified by the adoption of the Swiss Civil Code, the Nauckatel Civil Procedure Code and the Italian Penal Code. Egyptian law has been influenced by the French Codes and in Iraq the Islamic law and Ottoman law have been modified by the English commercial law. French law has had definite influence on the laws of Lebanon, Morocco, Tunisia and Algeria. A modern legal system was inacted in Persia (now Iran) in 1925-26 representing a compromise of Islamic law and Western codes and these codes have influenced Indonesian and Malayan law as well. Certainly the law of India has been influenced by the English common law, and a number of restatements of their law based on English common law have been adopted. Chinese law has been profoundly affected by Western influence for the past fifty years. Soviet law rests on early Russian law which was derived from Indo-European customs which are very similar to most European Codes. Russian law was greatly influenced by the Code Napoleon. The same is true for the development of the laws of Czechoslovakia, Hungary and Poland. Through the constant process of interaction, one on the other, the laws of nations have increased in their similarity to the point that today stripped of their procedure and ritual they unquestionably reflect a common interest and concern on which to build an effective modern world legal system to cope with the problem of international warfare.

As to modern Soviet justice, the comments of a professor of law at Duke University, on returning from a trip to Russia, are interesting: "Since ours was a group of lawyers, we were particularly concerned with Soviet justice. It is only fair to comment that we were favorably impressed with the professional ability of the Russian court officials and lawyers. While the court procedure is very unlike that in the United States and England, I found it quite similar to that which I had observed in Germany and elsewhere in western Europe.

"Many Russians freely admit that prior to the death of Stalin in 1953, many people had disappeared without trial or had been secretly tried in special courts of the MVD (secret police). They contended, however, that now these injustices have ceased. It was my conclusion that in a trial for a crime which had no political implications—something like larceny or assault—a Russian today would receive a fair trial and a fair sentence."[9]

NATO, CENTO, SEATO, OAS, the European Common Market and the Council of Europe are not to be confused with the need of a truly representative world institution to enact and interpret world law. Generally these organizations exist for economic or military reasons, whereas the United Nations' first responsibility is to secure a just international peace and to de-emphasize, not promote, the build-up of armaments.

Since international warfare involves the social conscience of the entire world community, only an organization representative of all nations can speak with authority and effectiveness in dealing with this problem.

The United Nations has been effective in the establishment of world standards and practices in the fields of agriculture, world health, international financing, international civil aviation, postal service, telecommunications, meteorology, maritime transportation and international labor practices among its other accomplishments. Yet, it is generally acknowledged that the United Nations as it is presently constituted has not prevented nor even curbed

9. From an article by Robinson O. Everett, Raleigh *News and Observer*, October 23, 1960.

the diabolical buildup of devices of mass destruction. It is this expenditure of the wealth of nations for purposes diametrically opposed to the welfare of the international society—that even threatens its very existence—that must come under the control of the United Nations and treated by the UN as a crime of the first magnitude against the peace of the world.

World peace will not be achieved without world government. Treaties, such as the limited nuclear test ban treaty, can serve mankind well as stepping stones to peace, but treaties alone have been tried with the tragic results of two world wars to prove their long range ineffectiveness. In August of 1928, the Kellogg-Briand Peace Pact was signed. Under its terms the high contracting parties agreed to renounce war as an instrument of national policy. Practically every nation in the world including all of the then major powers signed the treaty in which they agreed that the "settlement or solution of all disputes or conflicts of whatever nature or of whatever origin they may be, which may arise among them, shall never be sought except by pacific means." Within less than fifteen years the world was at war again. In spite of this bitter experience, there are still those who cling to the notion that arms cutbacks, truces and treaties can bring world peace. The fate of the League of Nations and the Kellogg-Briand Peace Pact should have shown man that he must not place his hopes for world peace on treaties without the cohesive and enforcing power of an independent, strong international political institution. There is simply no substitute for law and government in any peaceful society. This is no less true for nations than for states, counties, and towns where no thinking citizen would suggest that we could maintain order without federal, state and local law and government. Just as surely, we cannot free our world society from the disorder of international warfare without world law and government.

If the United Nations is then to become genuinely effective in its primary purpose, which is to maintain peace and remove threats thereto,[10] then the UN must become an instrument of law. It must contain within itself the power to enact and enforce law in the field of war prevention. Lacking this power it will fail in its primary purpose and become a forum for political histrionics when the major powers threaten the peace, and the tremendous humanitarian potential of the United Nations will continue to be only partially realized. But most importantly, the UN's potential as a preventative to human annihilation will go by default. That this does not happen must be the primary concern of the citizens of every nation.

10. United Nations Charter, Article 1, Section 1.

"It will be just as easy for nations to get along in a republic of the world as it is for you to get along in the republic of the United States. Now when Kansas and Colorado have a quarrel over the water of the Arkansas River, they don't call out the National Guard in each state and go to war over it. They bring a suit in the Supreme Court of the United States and abide by the decision. There isn't a reason in the world why we cannot do that internationally."

—HARRY S. TRUMAN

INTERNATIONAL COURT
OF JUSTICE

Prior to the first Hague peace conference, there had been for many years judicial settlements effected by arbitration between nations.[1] Such settlements were not infrequent and resulted from multilateral and bilateral treaties and conventions which provided for arbitration. Under the terms of the first Hague conference held in 1899, mediation and an international commission of inquiry, and arbitration were provided for nations at the world level as well as a panel of jurists called the Permanent Court of Arbitration. This was not to be a court in any sense, but rather each signatory power to the convention appointed four members; from this group nations desiring arbitration could choose competent arbitrators.

Our Secretary of State at the time, Elihu Root, recognized that procedures for arbitration were not sufficient and that there was need for a permanent tribunal composed of judges "who are judicial officers and nothing else, who are paid adequate salaries, who have no other occupations and who will devote their entire time to the trial and decision of international causes by judicial methods and under a sense of judicial responsibility."

1. See article by Louis B. Sohn, Professor of Law at Harvard University, appearing in the *American Bar Association Journal*; Vol. 46; January, 1960.

The second Hague conference held in 1907 revised the provisions of the 1899 conference, prepared and recommended to the powers represented a draft convention to establish an international court to be composed of judges elected for fixed periods who would be paid a fixed salary. Although the powers did not act directly on this proposal, the conference was influential in the subsequent development of the world court at a later date by the League of Nations.

Article 14 of the Covenant of the League of Nations provided:

> The Council shall formulate and submit to the Members of the League for adoption plans for the establishment of a Permanent Court of International Justice. The Court shall be competent to hear and determine any dispute of an international character which the Parties thereto submit to it. The Court may also give an advisory opinion upon any dispute or question referred to it by the Council or by the Assembly.

Pursuant to this article, in February of 1920 a committee of jurists was appointed to prepare the plans for a world court to be submitted to the League for consideration. These recommendations in a modified form were adopted by the League in December of 1920 and by September of 1921 the draft covenant, having been approved by the necessary majority of member nations, became the Statute of the Permanent Court of International Justice. This Court first met at The Hague in January of 1922 and met annually thereafter holding its last meeting in October of 1945, the year the United Nations and the present International Court of Justice came into being.

While the world court created by the League of Nations was in existence, it rendered twenty-three judgments and twenty-seven advisory opinions. The court did not have compulsory jurisdiction over the members of the League. Members—even non-members named in the Annex to the Covenant—were free to use the court or not as they saw fit. However, as in the case of the present world court, nations could file declarations in which they set forth the extent to which they recognized the jurisdiction of the court. Some twenty-nine nations accepted the compulsory jurisdiction of the court in varying forms and for differing periods of time.

The United States never became a member of the League of Nations world court although Secretaries of State Charles E. Hughes, Frank B. Kellogg and Henry L. Stimson together with Presidents Warren G. Harding and Herbert Hoover encouraged our joining with other nations in this effort to adjudicate international disputes peacefully. In January of 1935, a Senate resolution seeking to have the United States become a member of the world court failed to obtain the needed two-thirds vote of approval and no further action was taken to bring the U.S. into the court. Interestingly enough, James B. Moore, Charles E. Hughes, Frank B. Kellogg and Manley O. Hudson, all citizens of the United States, served as judges on the court even though our nation never became a party to the statute of the court.

When the League of Nations was supplanted by the United Nations, the Permanent Court of International Justice was replaced by the present International Court of Justice. Although the United States had refused to sanction our membership in the world court under the League of Nations, our participation in the International Court of Justice under the United Nations was unanimously approved by the Senate. After a sufficient number of nations had approved the statute of the International Court of Justice, it officially came into being and held its first session at The Hague in April of 1946.

The present world court does not have full jurisdiction over all legal disputes between member nations. Its jurisdiction is governed by the states themselves who, through declarations filed with the Secretary General of the United Nations, set forth the extent to which they agree to be bound by decisions of the court and over what period of time these agreements shall extend. This is similar to the situation that obtained in the old world court under the League of Nations.

Non-member nations may use the court under conditions to be laid down by the Security Council. Under the terms of the Statute of the International Court of Justice, these conditions must not place the parties to an international dispute in an unequal position before the court.

When the establishment of the present world court was being considered, it was strongly urged that the court be given compulsory jurisdiction so that any state could bring an action against any other state without the latter's consent. For fear that insistence on this idea would jeopardize the acceptance of the statute of the court by the requisite number of nations, the plan for compulsory jurisdiction was abandoned. In its place Article 36 of the Statute of the International Court of Justice was adopted whereby nations could file with the Secretary General of the United Nations a declaration setting forth the extent of their acceptance of the compulsory jurisdiction of the court.

These acceptances are often qualified. For example, France excepts disputes arising out of a crisis affecting her national security or out of any measure or action relating thereto. Britain reserves the right to terminate its acceptance on notice to the Secretary General, such notice to take effect from the moment of notification. Britain also reserves the right to add to, amend or withdraw her declaration. Generally British commonwealth nations reserve the right to withdraw their acceptance of jurisdiction on notice. Britain has a provision, also, to the effect that nations bringing suits against her must have accepted the court's compulsory jurisdiction for at least one year prior to bringing suit.

The United States has agreed to accept the compulsory jurisdiction of the world court with the provision that we can withdraw our acceptance on six months' notice. In addition, we have the famous and much discussed Connally Amendment to our acceptance of the court's jurisdiction which declares that the United States does not recognize the jurisdiction of the court in matters which are essentially within the domestic jurisdiction of the United States of America "as determined by the United States." This reservation was without precedent when it was enacted, but has since been adopted by many other nations. These six quoted words in effect make the United States judge of whether or not the world court has jurisdiction in every case in which the U.S. is involved. It is unheard of in the field of jurisprudence for a party to a legal dispute to rule on the jurisdiction of the trial court which is to hear and decide the matter in controversy. But the Connally Amendment in effect violates this legal maxim that a litigant shall not be judge in his own case. Thus, now when a matter comes before the world court in which our nation is named a party, all we need do is to determine unilaterally that the matter concerns our "domestic jurisdiction" and the case will be dismissed. Somewhat similarly, an action against France would presumably be dismissed if the French were to decide that it arose out of a crisis affecting or related to its national security. As to Britain and the commonwealth nations, an adverse judgment against one of these nations would ostensibly not be complied with after a withdrawal of its declaration of acceptance of compulsory jurisdiction, since such withdrawal takes effect the moment of notification under the terms of British participation in the world court.

Article 36(2) of the Statute of the International Court of Justice provides that the Court shall have jurisdiction of cases which are referred to it by the parties to the Statute and which concern: (*a*) the interpretation of a treaty; (*b*) any question of international law: (*c*) the existence of any fact which if established would constitute a breach of an international obligation; (*d*) the nature of extent of the reparation to be made for the breach of an international obligation.

Further, the Charter of the United Nations, of which the Statute of the International Court of Justice is an Annex, states in Article 2(7):

> Nothing contained in the present Charter shall authorize the United Nations to intervene in matters which are essentially within the domestic jurisdiction of any state or shall require the members to submit such matters to settlement under the present Charter; but this principle shall not prejudice the application of enforcement measures under Chapter VII. [Chapter VII deals with threats to the international peace and security.]

Thus, the jurisdiction of the International Court of Justice is confined to matters of international law, both by the Charter of the United Nations and by the Statute of the International Court of Justice. The Connally Amendment—the reservation to our nation's acceptance of the jurisdiction of the world court—is unnecessary because the court patently has no domestic jurisdiction in the first place. The Connally Amendment serves, as do other reservations to the compulsory jurisdiction of the court, to lessen the Court's prestige and influence and to degrade its power because it evidences a lack of faith in the ability of the court to do its appointed task and confine itself to matters of international law.

At the very least, the United States should repeal the Connally reservation and substitute a provision accepting the compulsory jurisdiction of the Court with respect to the interpretation of international agreements; such matters being clearly not within our nation's domestic jurisdiction.

As a legal matter, Connally-type reservations are probably not valid under international law because of the provisions of Article 36(6) of the Statute of the International Court of Justice which says: "In the event of a dispute as to whether the court has jurisdiction, the matter shall be settled by the decision of the court."

No Communist nation as of the time of this writing has accepted the compulsory jurisdiction of the international Court of Justice. Since Russia and other Communist members of the United Nations are automatically members of the world court, would this not work to the disadvantage of that non-Communist nation accepting compulsory court jurisdiction? The answer is found in the Norwegian Loans Case[2] in which the world court decided that unless both nations to a dispute had accepted the compulsory jurisdiction of the court without reservation, the action involved would be dismissed on motion of the

2. France vs. Norway; Case of Certain Norwegian Loans Issued in France (1957) I.C.J. Reports 5.

nation accepting compulsory jurisdiction. This means that if the United States were to take the lead in strengthening the world court by accepting compulsory jurisdiction without reservation, it could throw any nation out of court that had not also fully accepted the court's jurisdiction.

Since its inception in 1945, the present world court has dealt with twenty-nine contentious cases. During this time the court has shown no disposition to expand its jurisdiction beyond that set forth in its statutory mandate. For example, nineteen of the twenty-nine contentious cases were dismissed on admissibility or jurisdictional grounds. Former Ambassador Philip C. Jessup, onetime professor of international law and himself a member of the world court, said: "A study of the jurisdiction of the International Court of Justice reveals that . . . the Court has not shown the slightest inclination to amplify its own authority or to act in any but a judicial and impartial way."

By virtue of Article 2 of the Statute of the International Court of Justice, the judges must "possess the qualifications required in their respective countries for appointments to the highest judicial offices, or are jurisconsults of recognized competence in international law."

An exhaustive analysis by the Duke World Rule of Law Center has shown that there is "no noticeable difference in their [the judges] votes or opinions on particular issues attributable to differences in legal systems of the judges' countries. Most of the judges are versed in several legal systems. All are experts in the uniform system of law which the court's Statute requires it to apply—international law."[3]

3. *Questions and Answers on The World Court and the United States,* by Arthur Larson, Duke University, 1961.

Of the issues that have been decided by the Court, 103 known votes by national judges have been made public. In twenty-four of these, one or more of the judges has voted against the position advocated by his own nation because he thought his nation's position to be wrong; this includes judges from the Communist nations. There are fifteen instances in which the votes of judges from Communist nations have contradicted each other. In the Corfu Channal Case, two judges from Communist countries, Zoricic and Winiarski, voted against Albania, a Communist country, and in favor of Great Britain. In the Interhandel Case, the Russian judge, Kojevnikov, voted for the United States on three of the five issues before the Court. On one of these issues, the United States judge, Hackworth, voted against our position while the Russian judge voted in our favor.

The fear, then, that "foreign" and "Communist" judges would fail to rule justly and fail to render decisions based on the merits of a particular case has been proven false; such notions being absolutely without foundation in fact.

Judges on the world court do not represent the nations from which they are selected; they represent the entire world community. They are neither selected nor nominated by their home countries, but rather by groups in the Permanent Court of Arbitration. In the case of nations that are not members of the Court of Arbitration, appointment is made by national groups selected by their governments with careful attention to remove the nominations as nearly as possible from political consideration.

After the nominations are in, the task of electing the judges proceeds. Voting is carried out in the Security Council and the General Assembly of the United Nations. The electors are instructed to consider not only the qualifications of the prospective judges, but every effort is made to secure judges so that the court as a whole will represent the main forms of civilization and so that the principal legal systems of the world will be represented. In order to be elected, a nominee for a world court judgeship must receive an absolute majority of votes in both the Security Council and in the General Assembly. After election a judge is prohibited from engaging in any political or administrative function or to engage in any other professional activity, and before he assumes his office each judge must declare in open court that he will exercise his powers impartially and conscientiously.

While the court is composed of fifteen judges elected for nine-year terms, nine judges constitute a quorum. But as a practical matter all judges sit on every case unless a judge has been disqualified by reason of prior involvement in a particular case or in instances in which a judge is unable to attend due to illness. Should a case come before the court in which a nation is a party having no representation among the judges, that nation may select a judge to sit on the bench of the world court in the adjudication of its legal problem, but in any event no two judges may be nationals of the same country.[4]

It is clear that the Statute of the International Court of Justice and the Charter of the United Nations seek to maintain a court free from bias, and that the history of the court fails to support the fear that "foreigners" and "Communists" follow the dictates of their national governments rather than the equities of the questions presented for their determination.

The reasons generally advanced in support of restrictions on the Court's jurisdiction usually are based on imaginary fears unsupported by citations to judicial prec-

4. Statute 9 of the International Court of Justice; Article 3 (1).

dent, history or legal writings. These fears generally regard matters of domestic concern which, it is thought, might someday be ruled on by a court that does not exist, made up of unheard of judges lacking legal training, applying "laws" bearing no resemblance to international law.[5]

Today, and in the future, international law should have its supreme court. The basis of this tribunal must not rest on the shifting sands of self-judging reservations filed periodically with the Secretary General of the United Nations, but the court's jurisdiction and writ should be determined by the court itself under the provisions of the Statute which constitutes its mandate. It is untenable for the world court's jurisdiction to be a wavering, unsteady, ever changing matter subject to speculation among legal writers and to the whim of its member nations.

It is then suggested that an effective court must have equal jurisdiction over those subject to its writs. This concept is patently incompatible with unilateral jurisdictional determination by individual national units as exemplified by the United States' Connally reservation. The validity of these reservations is based on the premise that nations can in fact limit the jurisdiction of the court. While certainly under Article 36 of the Statute there is provision for the filing of declarations recognizing the jurisdiction of the court, the effect of these declarations is subject to further interpretation. These declarations and the provisions of the Statute for their filing should be interpreted by the court as merely a means whereby nations can openly declare their respect for the world rule of law as promoted by the court. The matter of ultimate jurisdiction particularly in matters which concern international peace should be determined finally by the court.

5. See article by Arthur Larson in the *American Bar Association Journal*, Vol. 46, No. 7, July, 1960.

This is in keeping with legal principle recognized throughout the civilized world.

Article 36(1) and (6) should be given interpretation
consistent with its language. Article 36(1) says, "The
Jurisdiction of the court comprises all cases which the
parties refer to it and all matters specially provided for
in the Charter of the United Nations or in treaties and
conventions in force." Is not the Charter itself a treaty or
convention in force? This document has been ratified by
the governments of well over one hundred nations of the
world, and since every member nation is also a party to
the Statute of the International Court of Justice these
nations should stand equally before the court and equally
subject to its jurisdiction.[6]

Again, Article 36(6) of the Statute states, "In the
event of a dispute as to whether the Court has juridiction,
the matter shall be settled by the decision of the Court."
This language is plain enough. It is for the Court itself
to take cognizance of those matters that come before it which involve international law or threaten the
effectiveness of the United Nations in carrying out the
purposes for which it was created. The UN's first purpose, as set forth in Chapter 1, Article 1(1), is: "To
maintain international peace and security, and to that end;
to take effective collective measures for the prevention
and removal of threats to the peace, and for the suppression of acts of aggression or other breaches of the
peace, and to bring about by peaceful means, and in conformity with the principals of justices and international
law, adjustment or settlement of international disputes or
situations which might lead to a breach of the peace."

It is the concern of every human being that the court
be an effective legal instrument in the carrying out of this
United Nations' purpose. This is the court's principal

6. United Nations Charter, Chapter XIV, Article 93 (1).

reason for existence. It is now time for the world court to act on its mandate and refuse to have its effectiveness in matters concerning world peace dissipated by reservations to its jurisdiction filed with the Secretary General. This action by the court is necessary if the United Nations is to succeed in its mission of securing for mankind a just peace under a rule of law.

"For I dipt into the future, far as human eye could see,
Saw the Vision of the world, and all the wonder that
would be;

Saw the heavens fill with commerce, argosies of magic
sails,
Pilots of the purple twilight, dropping down with costly
bales;

Heard the heavens fill with shouting, and there rain'd a
ghastly dew,
From the nations' airy navies grappling in the central
blue;

Far along the world-wide whisper of the south-wind rushing warm,
With the standards of the people plunging thro' the
thunder-storm;

Till the war-drum throbb'd no longer, and the battle-flags
were furl'd
In the Parliament of man, the Federation of the world.

There the common sense of most shall hold a fretful
realm in awe
And the kindly earth shall slumber, lapt in universal
law."

—ALFRED LORD TENNYSON
from *Locksley Hall*

THE FUTURE OF THE UNITED NATIONS

The alternative to an effective world organization is the domination of the world by either East or West probably preceded by World War III. Making the United Nations into an effective governmental organization with sufficient judicial, legislative and executive powers to prevent World War III is an imperative. The idea for the creation of such an international organization is no more novel today than was the idea for the creation of the nation state in the evolution of man's society. The admonition that no state can exist without a code, a court and a cop is no less valid than euphonious. The fate of the world must no longer be left to the whim of heads of state and foreign ministers. Summit conferences, cocktail diplomacy and unenforceable treaties are not substitutes for law and order.

Chapter Seven, Article 47 of the United Nations Charter provides for the establishment of a Military Staff Committee to advise and assist the Security Council relative to the military requirements of the maintenance of peace. It is to be the function of the Committee to employ and command forces placed at its disposal, to regulate armaments and possible disarmament. This Committee should become an active functioning organization and vital arm of the United Nations. The full force of the United Nations should be put into the effort to get nations to commit units of their armed forces to the Military Staff Committee. It is highly important that these national units be given international status with their primary allegiance to the world organization.

The decision of Denmark, Norway and Sweden to establish a 3,000-man Scandinavian unit available to the United Nations constitutes a beginning toward the fulfilment of the need for a ready world security force reserve. Hopefully many other nations will soon follow this commendable example of world co-operation in the cause of peace.

In addition, the United Nations of the future should be empowered to create its own security force. Here again the United States could show to the world its leadership and faith in the United Nations and world law by permitting its young citizens to enlist directly in United Nations service as an alternative to serving in the armed forces of this country. The United States would thereby offer a moral alternative to those of its young people who feel that military service to one nation is incompatible with the Christian ethic and the world rule of law.

There is a great misconception relative to regional arrangements fostered by the United States' action in the Cuban crisis under OAS sanction and by the Russian intervention in Hungary under the Warsaw Pact provisions. Each nation cited Article 52 of the Charter to justify its actions. Article 52 states "Nothing in the present Charter precludes the existence of regional arrangements or agencies for dealing with such matters relating to the maintenance of international peace and security as are appropriate for regional action. . . ." But these nations have conspicuously avoided citing Article 53 of the Charter which states in part, ". . . no enforcement action shall be taken under regional arrangements or by regional agencies without the authorization of the Security Council. . . ." It is plain from a reading of the Charter that where military action is contemplated the Security Council should be notified before such action is taken. While the right of self-defense is recognized in international law, this right cannot be used to justify aggression as was clearly set forth in the findings of the Nuremburg and Tokyo tribunals.

The General Assembly of the United Nations should create an international non-military force dedicated to the alleviation of those economic and social burdens of mankind that foment war. Again, countries should be urged to permit their young citizens to enlist directly in this effort, and time spent in service to this cause should be deducted from the required military service to their country.

Our nation's advocacy of such a force would deal a severe blow to the contentions that the United States' international concern is merely to recruit adherents to our side in the cold war, and would show our dedication to the achievement of world-wide solutions to common world problems.

The International Law Commission of the United Nations has endorsed the setting up of a world judicial agency with criminal jurisdiction. Clearly a system of district world courts to augment the activities of the International Court of Justice must be created. Such regional courts should be affiliated with the International Court of Justice. This is not to minimize the desirability of un-affiliated regional courts such as the European Court of Justice for the European Coal and Steel Community, the European Economic Community (Common Market) and the Atomic Energy Community (Euratom). Specialized courts of this type designed to interpret the terms of specific international treaties can greatly assist the peaceful international activities of nations. However, to try to substitute such specialized courts for a general system of district courts related to the International Court of Justice would tend to fragmentize the continued development of an international common law. The International Law Commission itself should be placed on a full-time basis. The Commission now meets only about ten weeks each year. The codification and development of international law is far too urgent a matter to be treated on a part-time basis.

Membership In UN

The question of membership in the United Nations should be determined only after full discussion by the General Assembly. The record of the United States in blocking the discussion of the entry of the Chinese Peoples Republic into the world body places us in a rather untenable position. We have in the past in effect said to the world that we are fearful to have the question of China's representation fully discussed by the members of the United Nations. Hopefully, our position on this matter has now changed. The question of whether a contending government should or should not be admitted to the UN should, at the very least, be fully discussed in the General Assembly. In the future a government should be admitted to the United Nations on the basis of a recommendation by the Security Council with the approval of the General Assembly. Such recommendations should not be allowed to be stymied by the veto of one nation as is presently possible. Further, the veto should be eliminated in all matters involving the peace of the world, including the election of the Secretary General.

In the future all nations should by the very fact of their existence be members of the United Nations. Nations then being ipso facto members of the United Nations of the future, the Security Council and General Assembly would simply be required to determine which of several contending governmental factions actually represents a particular nation. Under such a changed procedure, there would be no further self-defeating deliberations on whether or not an existing nation would be admitted to the United Nations. There would be no provision for a nation to withdraw its membership from the world body thus insuring every nation a voice in world affairs.

The carrying on of its world peace and humanitarian efforts has constantly placed the United Nations on the verge of bankruptcy. This hardly befits the dignity of so important an organization and unquestionably the United Nations of the future must have its own means of raising revenue. The best method would be to tax each national unit according to the value of its gross national product. This would not in turn mean increased taxes for individual citizens as monies now spent for tremendous national war machines would be shared by the United Nations in part and in part by individual citizens in the form of tax savings.

Since the per capita federal tax runs around $350.00 in the United States, 75 per cent of which is spent for war-related purposes, and since the per capita cost of the United Nations to our citizens is about $.67, it is apparent that our present emphasis is on war and not peace when three-fourth's of the federal tax dollar is spent for consequences of past wars and in the preparation for future wars. A return to peace-oriented production by the nations of the world would release large sums of money both for greater UN support and for tax savings by the nationals of its member states.

As presently constituted the General Assembly is made up of nations each having one vote. For example, the United States has a population one thousand times that of Iceland, yet each of these nations has one vote. It is obvious that the larger nations may in time not agree to be bound by decisions of the General Assembly in which they have been outvoted by a group of countries having only a small population and proportion of the resources of the world.

It has been suggested and recommended that each nation be permitted one to thirty representatives depending on an individual nation's population.[1] Each representative to the General Assembly would be entitled to one vote; each representative voting as an individual and all the votes of one nation would not have to be the same. There would thus be developed a spirit of representation of the world as a whole rather than of any particular nation. A representative could vote his personal judgment as to the best interests of all the peoples of the world. This would be similar to the situation that obtains in national parliaments where the interests of the whole nation are usually regarded as of no less importance than the interests of any particular group or locality. Under such an arrangement, a majority of the representatives to the UN would be required for the passage of all legislation. Presently, a two-thirds vote is required for passage of resolutions of great importance.

The formula for determining the number of representatives of any state might be as follows:

1. *World Peace Through World Law* by Clark and Sohn, Harvard University Press, 1958, pp. 52.

(1) Thirty representatives from any state with a population of over 140 million.

(2) Sixteen representatives from any state having a population of over 40 million, but not over 140 million.

(3) Eight representatives from any state having a population of over 20 million, but not over 40 million.

(4) Five representatives from any state having a population in excess of 5 million, but not over 20 million.

(5) Three representatives from any state having a population of over 1.5 million, but not over 5 million.

(6) Two representatives from any state having a population of over 500,000, but not over 1.5 million.

(7) There would be one representative from any nation having a population of not over 500,000.

The world population would be determined by a census taken under the supervision of the United Nations. Current population figures would be used until a UN census could be completed. Under the present census figures the foregoing formula, suggested by Clark and Sohn, would create a General Assembly membership of some 650 representatives.[2]

A UN of universal membership and increased authority would be the logical instrument for the settling of border disputes, a constant source of conflict between nations. Both the judicial and quasi-judicial (arbitration) elements of the United Nations could be used in the clarification of national boundary lines.

2. *Ibid.*

Individual responsibility for the maintenance of international peace initiated by the Nuremburg and Tokyo trials must figure prominently in the future of the United Nations.[3] Individual international criminals must be subject to arrest and tried in the district courts of the United Nations before whole innocent populations become involved in war.

The United Nations must have inspection forces with free access everywhere to detect possible violation of arms control. Individuals impeding the activities of these inspection committees must be summarily dealt with by UN district courts. It would be the function of the district courts to interpret the Charter of the United Nations and to pass on the propriety of measures passed by the General Assembly. Litigants should, of course, be given the right to appeal from the district courts to the International Court of Justice.

There is merit in the suggestion that an expanded and veto-free Security Council become the executive branch of the United Nations responsible to the General Assembly.[4]

One of the benefits of a stronger United Nations would be to lessen the fear of international war so as to permit us to rid our industry of many controls, priority and trade restrictions now presumably required for defense needs. We would not have to be constantly on guard for fear that some of our national products would fall in the hands of the "enemy." Savings from armament production could be applied to the needs of underdeveloped areas, a term which can well be applied to some parts of our own nation. These savings in the form of reduced taxes would increase purchasing power and demand for

3. See Appendix B, this volume.
4. *How To Give The United Nations Power To Enforce World Peace Through Law*, United World Federalists, Hartford, Connecticut.

consumer goods, needs and services which would in turn stimulate the world economy.

A United Nations empowered to keep the peace would permit our youth to plan their careers and their domestic lives free from the uncertainties attendant to the present balance of terror between nations. There would be a relaxing of tensions around the world. Each national crisis would not then become an international crisis. Disengagement of the major powers could be safely effected and a secure cessation of the current mad dash to nuclear destruction could be realized.

These are the areas in which the United Nations must develop if it is to become an effective instrument for a just and secure peace. Whether this development takes the form of self assertion as in the case of the Uniting For Peace Resolution or whether these changes must be effected by Charter review remains to be seen. It is likely that both methods will be employed. In any event the United Nations itself must not default in the process in its own responsibility to the world. It can and must evolve from within itself and grow by its own effort where its mandate permits as in the matter of strengthening the world court.

The calling of a conference to change the United Nations Charter is not subject to the veto. If a majority of the member nations approve a proposal to change the UN Charter, then this matter will be presented to the member nations for ratification. A proposal to change the Charter made at such a conference is also not subject to the veto. Changes recommended at a review conference would then be submitted to the member nations of the UN for their consideration and ratification. It is only at this stage that the veto could be used under the terms of the present Charter. After endorsement by two-thirds of the members of the United Nations, including all the five permanent members of the Security Council, a proposed Charter change would come into effect. Thus, a change or changes in the structure of the United Nations through the holding of a review conference, with the Charter requirement for ratification by two-thirds of the member states including all five permament members of the Security Council, would ultimately run into the problem of the veto. This points again to the desirability of the United Nations itself asserting its present authority under the Charter and under the Statute of the International Court of Justice to grow from within on its present mandate while at the same time seeking strenuously the holding of such a review conference when there appears reasonable prospect that such a conference would yield desirable proposals for Charter amendment.

If a review conference is held, it must not be assumed that the major powers will fail to ratify, or in effect veto, constructive proposals that may be presented for their adoption. Surely it would be foolish to prejudge a matter of such great moment and thus fail to try to strengthen the United Nations by charter revision.

Future Site For United Nations Headquarters

During the 1960 Fifteenth Session of the General Assembly of the United Nations, the UN was visited by Khrushchev, Castro, Kadar, Tito, Nassar, Nehru and other world leaders from abroad. Various factions in New York City demonstrated for and against their visits: Albanians, Greeks, Croats, Slovenes and Serbs, Spaniards and Hungarians, among others. These demonstrations were the largest in the city since the draft riots of 1863. A young Venezualean girl visiting in New York was shot and killed by a stray bullet from an anti-Castro faction.

Khrushchev's limousine was splattered with eggs; rocks were thrown through the back window of the Albanian premier's car and the Yugoslavian consul was severely kicked by an anti-Tito picket. In order to control the crowd, the New York police stood shoulder to shoulder from Pier 73, where Khrushchev landed in his ship Baltika, to his headquarters. In 1961 American Negroes in the balcony of the Security Council caused general disruption in the proceedings of that body's discussion of the vital Congo situation. Fist fights broke out and a generally chaotic scene was presented to the world largely caused by the action of United States citizens.

While these demonstrations and incidents do not in themselves constitute a reason for moving the United Nations Headquarters, they do point to a potential problem of tomorrow and the possibility that at a later time and under more severe tension when the free functioning of the UN would be most important, access to the UN Headquarters by foreign dignitaries and delegations might be made impossible due to the obstructionist tactics of nonsympathetic elements in this country. It is quite conceivable that the New York police in a time of greater tension could not insure the safety of movement of UN delegations and that the crowds themselves could, through an act of violence, cause an incident that would jeopardize world peace. There will always be the problem of getting the delegates physically into the United States and then to the United Nations. Very clearly New York City was not a place conducive to objective dispassionate discussions and visits between delegation headquarters during the Fifteenth General Assembly Session. During more trying times, discussions and visitations might well be rendered impossible and actions by the citizenry increase world tension at the worst possible moment.

In addition, the United Nations of the future will need a larger physical plant to house a more representative and democratically constituted General Assembly. It would be more desirable to have the United Nations located in an area apart from any major power and preferably on its own island territory where access could be had by delegates without crossing the boundaries of another nation. Formosa seems ideally situated for this purpose, and by making Formosa world territory both East and West could save face in this great trouble spot. A self governing world headquarters for the UN would give more stability to the world organization. Guam, Okinawa, Cyprus and Malta are but other areas that might be granted to the United Nations where free access by the representatives of all nations could be assured.

A prerequisite to the relocation of the United Nations would, of course, be the agreement through plebecite by the inhabitants of any proposed future UN site. As time passes, there may well arise a growing interest on the part of island areas with unclear national affiliation to become the seat of the world's government.

Wherever located, the UN of the future must grow in no small degree from within and by its own effort based on the authority it already has received from the peoples of the world. Charter review should be viewed as a desirable and needed adjunct to this process of inner growth, but it is very important that the self-strengthening powers inherent in its present mandate—particularly as to the creation of a strengthened world court system—be fully utilized by the United Nations in the years ahead.

"We discuss . . . the question of War and Peace . . . with words like coexistence, appeasement, preventive war. These are not the words of high politics. The great words of high politics are Liberty, Justice, and Law—Freedom under Law. These words will never be replaced as the basic stuff to human destiny. They must therefore be made to mean something in our age. If these words perish, even for a space, America will perish with them. But how much have intellectuals concerned themselves with this matter of Law in the world? What explorations have our Advanced Guard made into questions of Law as governing the relations of nations and all people within all nations? . . . Who among them is also trying to define for our age . . . the universal relationship between human law and ideal justice? It is a deep and prickly subject. Easier to ignore it. But like the Hound of Heaven, this question will pursue you—for the fact is: there can be no peace without law. Nor freedom either."

—HENRY R. LUCE

FREEDOM AND WORLD
GOVERNMENT

Sometimes world government is opposed on the grounds that all peoples do not share a common culture. The West is presented as the exemplary standard by which all others should live. Citation is made to indignities, injustices, aggressions and atrocities committed in Communist and non-Western nations to prove that it would be dangerous to enter a world government and relinquish a measure of our sovereignty to a government which contained representatives from Communist and non-Western lands.

Some individuals would readily accept a federation of NATO countries but at the same time shrink from joining with all nations in a government of the whole; albeit not all NATO countries share Western culture, but most do and there are no non-Western members of NATO that rank among the top powers of the world.

Then for the person considering the merits of the movement for world government, it becomes important to examine this legacy which we call "Western culture" and see if in fact it has not contributed its share to the sum total of human misery of both a political and economic nature.

The doctrine of laissez faire of Adam Smith—which sometimes finds expression in the shorthand phrase "that

government governs best that governs least"—is not now
and has probably never been practiced as a practical matter
either here or abroad. In its absolute terms it was, in fact,
never susceptible of application, and while containing in it
great economic power when applied in modified form, it
also can be used—and certainly in the early years of the
industrial revolution was used—as a means of rationaliz-
ing governmental indifference to human misery. Capitalism through a system of wider distribution of corporate
stock, social security and innumerable governmental controls has moved us leagues away from capitalism as it was
originally conceived and into a system of government
more akin to modern socialism. Certainly it cannot be contended that a government that tells farmers what to
plant, sets prices, enters business, insures its citizens against
all manner of difficulties, conscripts its youth, confiscates a
great portion of individual and corporate earnings in the
form of taxes—surely this is not a laissez faire or let-alone
economy under which we live in the United States. The
influence of Bentham, Dickens and Marx, among many
others, has had its effect and in truth there has been a
revolution in America and the workers do share in large
measure in the fruits of their labor. This has come about
through the labor union movement and the ballot box;
it is a good thing in the main, but it is surely not moribund
capitalism that we enjoy today in the United States. The
saga of America has been the steady march toward
freedom under this evolving system. Undoubtedly its
strength lies in its inherent tolerance of divergent ideas
and general dedication to spiritual freedom. Its weakness
lies in its loss of resources and freedoms to the false notion
that the war system brings us national security.

As the doctrine of laissez faire has given way to
liberalizing change in the United States, Marxism has

undergone changes in the Soviet Union. As the people were educated under their program of mass free education, the police state of the Stalin-Beria era began to fade. Communism in its pure form is now giving way to the practical solution of problems and the theory of government is less the concern of Communist nations than are means in which to increase production and to be effective competitors with other nations, both Communist and non-Communist, in securing a better way of life for their citizens.[1]

Communist nations by impounding large amounts of the production of their workers have violated the tenets of Marxism and have proceeded to establish a highly productive capital industry in an amazingly short time. Conversely, capitalist nations through the adoption of ways in which workers can share more abundantly in the goods they produce have often violated the academic theory of free enterprise capitalism. Thus, as an economic proposition, the two systems have moved closer together. This economic fact is, however, of strictly secondary moment. The matter of freedom of the individual is of supervening importance.

Aggression

As Americans we are sometimes guilty of feeling that we are the possessors of absolute truth and the Communists are absolutely wrong; that we have never been guilty of aggression against another country; do not covet the lands of other nations, and would not be guilty of subversion. But our history does not bear out such conclusions.

1. For a detailed discussion see: "Puzzling Question: What is a Communist?" by A. A. Berle, Jr., New York *Times Magazine*, December 19, 1960. Also, *The View From America* by Clinton Rossiter, Harcourt Brace, New York, 1960.

Certainly we took the beginnings of our nation from the American Indian by invasion and aggression. We obtained California, Texas, Utah, New Mexico and Colorado after sending Generals Zachary Taylor and Winfield Scott into Mexico where Scott captured Mexico City; Mexico thereafter ceded large areas of its land to the United States. Clearly Texas and California had been "infiltrated" by Americans prior to their loss to Mexico and Spain. Our acquisition of the Hawaiian Islands is a clear case of a sovereign kingdom being overthrown by infiltration.

The people of the Philippines have not forgotten that in 1889-90 the United States by military action overthrew their constitutional government and that the Philippines did not return to the status of a sovereign independent state until July 4, 1946. The Philippines, Guam and Puerto Rico were ceded to the United States as a result of the Spanish American War and the resulting Treaty of Paris of 1889, clearly accretion by conquest. In attempting to justify the annexation of the Philippine Islands by the United States, President McKinley declared that, "there was nothing left for us to do but to take them all, and to educate the Filipinos, and uplift and Christianize them as our fellowmen for whom Christ also died."

Cubans have not forgotten that their country was occupied by the United States, remained under our military rule from 1899 to 1902, and that one of the conditions of their freedom was that we be permitted to maintain naval stations on the island. Further, Cubans have not forgotten the thousand-pound bombs made in the United States, supplied by us to Batista, that fell on their revolutionary forces seeking to overthrow the Cuban dictatorship; nor will Cubans soon forget the subversion generated by the United States to overthrow the Castro regime. Similarly,

Algerians have not forgotten the French strafing of their open villages by Corsair fighter planes made in the United States, nor the Cypriots that their villages were strafed by the Turks using NATO jet fighters made in the United States, nor the Viet Namese that their villages were fire-bombed by United States aircraft.

The Russians have not forgotten that in 1918, with the assistance of the British, French and the Japanese, several thousand American troops invaded Russia landing at Murmansk, Valdivostock and Archangel, overthrowing the local Soviet government and setting up their own provisional government with the French occupying Odessa and with seven thousand United States troops guarding the Trans-Siberian railway. Nor will the Russians soon forget the deliberate over-flights by U-2 aircraft of the United States that were so forcefully brought to the world's attention in the spring of 1960.

The people of Japan are not impressed by our claims to having no extra-territorial intentions. They know that their prefecture of Okinawa is occupied by the United States, that while it has a local legislature, its chief executive is appointed by U.S. authorities and that the former capital city of Naha is now the seat of our military government of that island.

It was in 1958 that United States Marines were sent into Lebanon in an action that was said to have "the flavor of madness about it."[2] Again in November of 1960, units of the United States Navy were ordered to patrol the coast of Guatemala and Nicaragua to prevent the landing of troops and supplies from abroad. In commenting on this action, *El Tiempo*, Columbia's largest newspaper said, "It disturbs us profoundly that the action was taken without taking the Organization of American States into ac-

2. See: *The Nation*, August 2, 1958.

count and without even consulting other governments in the hemisphere." Mexico's *Ultimas Nopicias* said the action was inopportune and would provoke anti-Americanism in South America since the O.A.S. was not consulted.[3]

Slavery

Speaking at the Republican Convention in Chicago in the summer of 1960, Minnesota's Congressman Walter H. Judd declared that the issue before the world is once again slavery, but "this time not men enslaved by other men, but far more complex and dangerous, masses of men enslaved by governments." Repeatedly Americans hear that the choice confronting the world is freedom or slavery. Such statements presume that those who live under Communism live in a state of slavery. Statements of this type are irresponsible and untrue. Their basis stems largely from the days of mass exportations of Latvians, Estonians, Lithuanians and other political prisoners by the Russians to Siberia by the police state of the Stalin era. Now Russian concentration camps are being done away with and large numbers of prisoners returned to their homes. For example, the large Vorkuta labor camps are now closed as are those at Karaganda, having been replaced by housing projects. While it would be inaccurate to say that there are no political prisoners in Russia today, it would be just as inaccurate to say that Americans imprisoned under the Smith Act here in the United States are not political prisoners. In Russia there was a great stride toward personal liberty and an easing of tension under Khrushchev.[4] Liberty in the Soviet Union

3. New York *Times*, Section 4, November 20, 1960.
4. *To Moscow—And Beyond* by Harrison E. Salisbury, New York, 1960, pp. 20-24.

is an emerging, undeniable thing that should continue as the masses are educated and the government matures.

We in the United States should not lose sight of the fact that when our government was as young as the Russian government, we were buying and selling human beings. It was in England under William and Mary that the slave trade to the Americas and the West Indies was opened to all subjects of the crown. There were at that time 192 slave ships sailing from English ports. Later the slave trade was outlawed and British men-o-war sent out to hunt down vessels carrying slaves. There was a premium for any naval captain who could bring in one of these slave ships intact. In order to prevent discovery on the approach of a warship the slave ship captains often practiced atrocities to get rid of their load of slaves before capture. It is estimated that three times as many Negroes left Africa in slave ships after the trade was outlawed as before because it had become such a "good thing." Of all the Negroes that left Africa during this period, it is believed that two-thirds were murdered on the high seas. Since some two million slaves were imported into the British colonies, the barbarism of this segment of Western culture is apparent.

It then could be reasonably suggested that instead of hurling irresponsible charges of slavery at the Communist nations we had better address ourselves to the problem of slavery where it really exists today. For example, the old form of chattel slavery as once practiced in the United States is still found in Arabia. In 1936 King Ibn Saud made a decree regulating the condition of slaves and giving them the right to have their freedom under certain conditions. In 1953 the French Ambassador in Saudi Arabia informed his government that slave traders posing as Moslem missionaries were enticing Africans to accompany them to Mecca. On arrival in Saudi Arabia they were arrested for landing in the country without a visa and were turned over to slave traders who sold them into slavery.

Slavery is also found in Ethiopia today. In other parts of the world, men pledge their services or the services of someone under their control—possibly a child—as security for a debt. The value of the services are not thereafter credited toward the liquidation of the indebtedness and the person pledged remains enslaved for life.

Then if, as Americans, we are genuinely interested in securing freedom rather than building ill will against Communist nations, why do we not concern ourselves with those who are truly enslaved?

To pursue further the legacy of misdeeds that we have received from our Western culture, we should not forget that in England, the motherland of our common law, the burning of heretics was made legal in 1400. This law was once repealed but later revived in 1539 as a punishment for denying transubstantiation. Again in 1558, the burning of human beings was outlawed, but King Edward VI, James I and Elizabeth I continued to burn heretics anyway. Human burning was stopped in England in 1610, but the law of Scotland in the days of Charles II was to the effect that witches were to be "worried at the stake and then burnt," and in Europe countless numbers of "witches" were burned at the stake. As a matter of fact, laws were passed in Massachusetts at one time against Baptists; some were put to death while others were whipped and branded. At the same time throughout New England, hundreds were arrested and punished—even put to death—for witchcraft.

It was under the aegis and at the bidding of the Church that laymen during the Crusades indulged their belicose natures by riding off to kill in the name of the Lord. For such activity, the fighter was assured of perfect salvation and the remission of sins. It was at about this time that flagellation as a form of penance was practiced and for years the Church engaged in the sale of indulgences whereby a man could in effect buy off the devil himself by paying the going rate set by the church. What a shame it would be if the present Protestant and Catholic ecumenical movements were twisted to justify a military "holy crusade" to rid the world of Communism.

It was Western culture that produced Karl Marx, Adam Smith, Adolf Hitler and Benito Mussolini, Communism, Capitalism, Nazism and Fascism. The slaughter of the Jews in our Western society produced a new word —"genocide"—and a horrendous chapter in man's history which has no parallel. When extermination by mass shooting, starvation and disease proved too slow and expensive, the Germans, during World War II, designed and built gas chambers; bodies were removed from these chambers to adjacent crematories and consumed by fire. In this manner, about four million Jews were put to death at Oswiecim (Auschwitz), Mjdenik, Treblinka, Dauchau, Buchenwald, Bergen-Belsen and at other camps. The total number of Jews killed is conservatively estimated at 5,750,000.

Hitler's philosophy was, "mankind has grown strong in eternal struggles, and it will only perish through eternal peace."[5] Mussolini, too, reflected this Nietzsche-like reasoning when he wrote, "First of all, as regards the future development of mankind—and quite apart from all present political considerations—facism does not, generally speaking, believe in the possibility or utility of perpetual peace.

5. *Mein Kampf* by Adolf Hitler, Peynal and Hitchcock Edition, p. 175.

War alone keys up all human energies to their maximum tension, and sets the seal of nobility on . . . peoples."[6]

Yet, in spite of the West's declared opposition to these philosophies and the crimes against humanity committed in their name during World War II, the German armed forces since the war have been rebuilt by the West through the extensive use of former Nazi officers. This was done in the face of opposition even within West Germany where men in uniform after World War II were publicly booed. To climax what could well appear to neutral nations to be Western lack of concern with Nazi philosophy, German V-2 rocket experts were permitted to escape without trial as war criminals and brought to the United States to continue their work, while a former Nazi general staff officer close to Hitler, Adolph Heusinger, was named in 1960 as Chairman of NATO's Permanent Military Committee.

Before Hitler, in World War I, it was the West that first used chemical warfare. On April 15, 1915, a chlorine attack was launched against the Allied position in the Ypres salient. Yet prior to this attack the United States failed to support a measure to stop the use of gas in warfare presented at The Hague International Peace Conference of 1899. The reasons we gave were that the use of gas had not yet been proven inhumane and that such preventative measures to restrict inventiveness were not conducive to world peace. One of our delegates, Admiral Mahan, explained that asphyxiating gases could "produce decisive results" and were no worse than conventional firearms. In the Geneva Convention of 1925, forty-two countries agreed that gas warfare had been "condemned by a consensus of the civilized world" and agreed to prohibit the use of gas and bacteriological agents in war. The United States failed to enter this treaty.

6. See: *The Doctrine of Fascism* by Benito Mussolini, vol. XIV (1932) pp. 847-851, Enciciopedia Italiana.

It was the United States on August 6, 1945, that dropped the first nuclear bomb on an open city. As a result, most of the city of Hiroshima was destroyed and some 200,000 people killed. Only three days later 39,000 people were killed when the second nuclear bomb was dropped, this time on Nagasaki. Here there were an additional 25,000 people injured. People are still dying in Japan from the effects of these bombings. It should also be remembered that it was the United States and British fire-bombs that cremated over 100,000 civilians in air raids on Hamburg and Tokyo during World War II.

While the word "genocide" was conceived to describe the type of mass executions practiced by the Nazis, the word "lynching" has an American derivation. It is thought to have been derived from the name of a Virginian, Charles Lynch, who headed an organization during the Revolutionary War that punished thieves, outlaws, and Tories. In the southern United States vigilante committees tarred and feathered, flogged and hanged agitators who opposed slavery or assisted runaway slaves. After the Civil War such organizations as the Ku Klux Klan and the Order of the White Camellia intimidated former slaves out of the exercise of their civil rights and lynched an undetermined number of Negroes. Lynching was not confined to the South, however, as it was widely practiced in the frontier days in the West. It is said that only Rhode Island, Massachusetts, New Hampshire and Vermont have had no lynchings. The Negro Year Book has published figures (1951) compiled largely at Tuskegee Institute in Alabama, showing that between 1882 and 1951 4,730 persons were lynched in the United States; about two-thirds of these were Negroes.

One ugly episode in American history was the placing of 110,000 West Coast Japanese, most of whom were

American citizens, in concentration camps in the 1940's. After Pearl Harbor hatred for Japanese—all Japanese —ran deep in America. The Tennessee State Department of Purchasing declared "open season on Japs, no licenses required." An elderly Japanese couple was shot to death as they slept in their home in El Centro, California, victims of a super-patriot. Another such pathetic "patriot" began chopping down the cherry trees that ring the Tidal Basin in Washington.

Feeling against the Japanese continued to mount as the war continued. From the governor of California to the Native Sons and Daughters of the Golden West there came pressure to move our Nisei population from the Pacific Coast, ignoring their constitutional and civil rights. On February 19, 1942, this movement began under Executive Order 9006. The General's brother, Milton Eisenhower, was appointed director of the War Relocation Authority and the movement to concentration camps began. The order of evacuation included all persons of Japanese descent. It is interesting to note that the fear that generated the order was completely lacking in over-all logic, aside from its total lack of democratic process, because the Territory of Hawaii was not included in the order. 120,552 Japanese-American citizens were living in Hawaii at the time and not one single act of sabotage or espionage was claimed against any of these islanders.

California profiteers hastily bought up the valuable farm lands and businesses left by their Japanese-American neighbors. Lieutenant General John DeWitt was in charge of the areas evacuated and in an appearance before a Senate Committee said, "A Jap's a Jap. It makes no difference whether he's an American citizen or not."

The concentration camps for Japanese-Americans were located west of the Sierra Nevada mountains and had no inside plumbing. The tarpaper shacks were heated by only a single potbellied stove. Two families were crowded into each 20 foot by 25 foot "apartment." Watchtowers were installed at the edges of the camps and they had all the earmarks of Nazi stalags. After the war, the federal government indemnified these citizens only to the extent of one-third of the value of their property losses.

In referring to this black episode in our American history, Yale Professor, Eugene Rostow, wrote in 1945: "The evacuation was our worst wartime mistake. . . . One hundred thousand persons were sent to concentration camps on a record which wouldn't support a conviction for stealing a dog."

While our attention was being directed to the killings of the rebellious blacks in the Congo in 1963 and while most Americans held the view that the "uncivilized" Congolese did not deserve independence, little notice was given to the far greater atrocities in "civilized" white Portuguese Angola.

There, for example, an African woman nine months pregnant and the mother of three children was conscripted by the government in the forced-labor program to work on the roads. Unable to keep up, she was flogged to death. In the village of Mucucuiji, white civilians came in the middle of the night and herded all able-bodied black men of the town into a confinement area and shot them all. Pedro de Sousa and Franciso Manuel de Silva, black Christian priests, were killed in their churches by white mobs. Some native villages were totally destroyed by the Portuguese in retaliation against actions by the natives in seeking fair wages for their work in cotton fields controlled by a Portuguese Belgian firm. These villages were destroyed by fire bombings, the inhabitants burned alive. These fire bombs were marked "Property of the U. S. Air

Force" and were supplied to Portugal as a NATO part-
ner.[7]

In all, 150,000 black refugees from Portuguese terror
had to flee Angola. To remain meant to be exploited.
The African section of Luanda, the capital city, is a ghetto
of one-room huts where natives are often pulled from
their houses, shot and left in the streets. In all, 45,000
Africans have been killed for resisting inhuman treatment
by the government; it is a land devoid of human freedom
for 4 million blacks who are being terrorized by 200,000
Portuguese inhabitants.

It is to the everlasting credit of the United States that
Adlai Stevenson in March of 1961 spoke in support of a
motion to censure Portugal for its oppressive actions
against the Africans of Angola. This action in the United
Nations came late, but at least on the surface appeared
designed not to gain political advantage nor to gain rocket
bases abroad but rather to halt the suppression of a people
seeking basic human rights and freedom. This is in the
highest tradition of our nation. Our words were fine, but
what of our actions in supplying Portuguese Dictator
Antonio de Oliveria Salazar with fire bombs with which he
could and did burn men alive who were seeking freedom?
Was this an accident or had the same thing happened in
Cuba and in Algeria?

The treatment of the Negro in South Africa far
exceeds in its violation of human dignity and freedom
governmental restrictions in the Soviet Union or segregation in the United States. Apartheid, ironically pronounced "a-PART--hate," is segregation supported by the
state whereby there is one law for those of European
descent, another for the non-European. It is this system

7. See Associated Press dispatch from Nkambe-Miole, Angola; August
26, 1961.

that obtains for the 9,000,000 Africans in white-ruled South Africa. It pervades the lives of the African at home, at work, in school, and as he moves from place to place within his own town.

Johannes Oliphant, a middle-aged African, was tried in a Durban court for entering town to seek a job to support his family. He protested that he simply wanted to work. Six policemen dragged him out of court to serve sixty days in jail. Oliphant had not stayed in his place. The government of South Africa seeks to make urban areas as exclusively white as possible and to this end the movement of black men is rigidly controlled.

Each African must carry a small book of nearly one hundred pages which gives his name and tribe, his record and employer. He must carry this with him at all times under penalty of being turned over to a farmer where he is paid nine pence a day. With this income he is expected to pay the fine levied against him by the court for failure to produce his identification.

Louis Nkost, a twenty-three-year old African journalist, won a Nieman Fellowship to study at Harvard University. Two white men also from South Africa also won fellowships at the same time and were granted passports without difficulty. Nkost's application for a passport was not answered. He hired an attorney and was finally granted an "exit permit" which is given to citizens who are to leave the country and never return. Should Nkost return to his native land, he will be subject to prosecution.

There is a permanent curfew for Africans in all South African cities; generally business establishments are not open to these people in their own land. A commonly displayed sign in windows and on the walls of "public" and commercial establishments proclaims "Dogs And Natives Are Not Allowed."[8]

8. For an account of the treatment of the Negro in South Africa see:

While Americans were concerned over the headlines dealing with the Berlin and Cuban crises in 1962 and 1963, the United States was engaged in a secret war of great proportions. Under the terms of the 1954 Geneva accord, Viet Nam was to be independent from French rule and free from the introduction of armament by the signatory powers. But the United States committed over two billion dollars to shore up the corrupt government headed by President Ngo Dinh Diem. This government was historically corrupt and operated on a police-state basis. Opposition to the government was ruthlessly suppressed even when anti-Communist. In September of 1962, one hundred anti-Communist National Union Front members were jailed without trial for opposing Diem. Hundreds were imprisoned on the Island of Puolo Condore in the South China Sea for their anti-government activities and banished from their homeland without trial. Most of these men were anti-Communists.

The United States sent ten thousand soldiers to Viet Nam to "bring democracy" to the people. These soldiers were called "advisors" by the Pentagon. They succeeded in fortifying the villages and greatly increasing the ability of these people to kill their fellow countrymen. Our soldiers in their goading of the normally peaceful native population to a war effort did not endear us to the inhabitants of South Viet Nam. This is even true as to the Vietnamese soldiers who repeatedly stoned American military "advisors."[9]

The United States' involvement in Formosa is as flagrant a case of modern imperialism as could be

"The Human Meaning of Apartheid" by Nathaniel Nakasa, The New York *Times Magazine*, September 24, 1961.

9. See *Viet Nam: Conflict That Is Hush-Hush*, by Ben Price, Associated Press release from Washington of November 11, 1962.

imagined. The status of this island was to be formally determined after World War II by the Allied Powers. Such determination has never been made because Chiang Kai-shek, using squatter's rights, and the United States, using the Seventh Fleet, have in effect denied to the nations of the world a considered judgment of the future status of this island in what is a propaganda gem for the Chinese on the mainland.

Many Americans entertain the fiction that had we only given Chiang Kai-shek proper support while he was on the mainland, China would not have become a Communist nation. We fail to understand that he is an opportunist of the first order. Chiang was not supported by the Chinese people during the Chinese Civil War and he is much less popular today on the mainland.

In 1920 Chiang went to Moscow to meet Lenin, Trotsky and Chickerin and to study Bolshevist strategy. Chiang never became a Communist, but soon was assured of financial support from Shanghai bankers which enabled him to begin his career. We tend to look on Chiang as a great general and humanitarian. Such is not the case. He has never won a major military campaign which he personally directed. When on the mainland he had unwilling villagers conscripted, chained together and trudged off to training camps. Many of these villagers turned themselves and their equipment over to the Communists at the first opportunity. Much of the money that was sent by the United States to assist Chiang found its way into the pockets of his officers who, with Chiang, were hated by the Chinese people for the same reasons for which they were to be later hated by the Formosans.

When Chiang arrived on Formosa after his expulsion from China his troops looted stores and slaughtered thou-

sands of Formosans.[10] The top legislators in the government of Formosa were appointed by Chiang Kai-shek and
then elected by rigged elections in 1948. Many of these
Chinese Nationalists still hold their positions and control
the population which is 80 per cent Formosan. Seventy
per cent of the present army there is composed of Formosans who have been conscripted and who are not in the
least interested in recapturing the mainland of China.
This army serves two functions: (1) to get money from
the United States as a "bulwark against communism";
(2) to maintain Chiang's dictatorship over the island.
Chiang would not last a week without American assistance,
and we are committed to the defense of Formosa and the
Pescadores by treaty. The maintenance of Chiang on
Formosa and his nationalists on Quemoy and Matsu, only
a rifle shot from the Chinese mainland, not only constitutes colonialism in its rankest form, but affords the
Communist government of China strong support for their
claim that the United States has imperialist designs on
mainland China, and thereby enables the Chinese government to obtain from the people superhuman efforts of
production in order to defend their homeland against
"Yankee imperialism." The bitterness engendered by this
situation daily prolongs the day when China can be
brought under the world rule of law. Certainly this is no
where made more manifest than in our annual opposition
to the admission of representatives of China to the United
Nations. If there were ever a self-defeating foreign policy
concept it is that the United States supports its own interests and upholds international morality by opposing the
admission of true China to membership in the United
Nations.

10. See: *A Nation of Sheep* by William J. Lederer, Fawcett Publications, July, 1962.

The people of China—both on Formosa and on the mainland—regard Formosa as a province of China (T'aiwan sheng). Our protestations that we do not intervene in the affairs of other nations surely gets little sympathy from Chinese or Formosans as they see the Seventh Fleet of the United States interposed between Formosa and the mainland, preventing the Chinese from exercising dominion over their island.

While it is generally known that there have been monstrous political killings under the Chinese Communist government, it is not well known that millions of civilians were killed under the Chiang regime.[11] The essential point is that the people of China have had no supranational institutional representation to use in defense of these barbarisms committed by both the Chiang and Communist regimes. The world community has in effect walled out the Chinese people and we have done this in the name of morality. What a hopelessly inept approach to international justice to encourage the isolation of one fourth of the world's people! If the Chinese people are to be granted freedom, it will be under world law and not outside of it and surely not through nuclear bombardment. If the world is to free itself from the threat of Chinese militarism, it must permit and encourage the true Chinese government to participate in the discourse of nations and in the framing of world-level institutions of law and government to bring the consciousness of mankind to bear on the universal problems of war, proverty, illness and ignorance.

The case of Syngman Rhee is but another illustration of how we can be readily led down the garden path in the name of anti-Communism. Was not Syngman Rhee a venerable old patriot who hated Communism? Of course

11. *A Curtain of Ignorance* by Felix Green, Doubleday, 1964.

he was; he had even taken an American wife and had been tortured by Communists. Clearly these things ought to insure that he would be ideal to lead his nation to freedom against the Communists. So the argument ran. What we again failed to realize was that Rhee was a despot, a selfish, corrupt politician that did not represent human freedom. Under his rule a common thief would be punished by having his fingers broken. Anyone who politically opposed Rhee was a "traitor" and "Communist" and summarily arrested, often executed. The essential to political survival in Korea from 1948 until Rhee's expulsion by the people, was to agree with him. Bribery was rampant. In the elections held in 1952, Rhee's opponent for the presidency was unable to campaign and went into hiding for fear of his life. When the Taegu Mail attacked Rhee and his administration, the plant where the paper was published was wrecked by Rhee's henchmen. In 1956 ballot boxes mysteriously disappeared but in spite of this an opposition candidate was elected president. Later that year he was duly shot.

Our support of Syngman Rhee and later of General Pak in Korea is not unique. We have supported oppressive oligarchies in South Viet Nam, Indonesia, Formosa, Guatemala, Jordan, Iran, Nicaragua, Turkey, Spain, Portugal, and Pakistan in the name of anti-Communism. The tragedy lies in the fact that we have failed to see that we are supporting the very evils which we claim to oppose. We simply do not have the moral right or the economic capacity to determine the destiny of the nations of the earth. If we are truly interested in the rights of people, we must become dedicated to the creation of democratic international government wherein these rights can be protected under a rule of law.

In the United States, where human life is supposed to receive its highest dignity, capital punishment is still practiced in all but nine states. But the death penalty has fallen into disuse. Only a relative few of those convicted of capital crimes are executed. The evidence is that capital punishment is now used in a macabre form of discrimination reserved for the poor—particularly the poor Negro.

Is capital punishment a deterrent to murder and rape? The statistics would indicate the answer to be no. Of the ten states with the highest murder rate, nine still practice capital punishment. Of the ten states having the lowest murder rate five have abolished capital punishment. Nine of the ten states having the highest rape rate use capital punshment whereas five of the ten states having the lowest rape rate have abolished capital punishment.

It is then apparent that evidence fails to support the theory that capital punishment is essential to the control of the commission of the most heinous of crimes, i.e., murder and rape.

Finding the practices of capital punishment abhorrent, thirty nations have abolished it. The United States should join this group in the abolition of this uncivilized practice wherein governmental authority orders the destruction of human life. Capital punishment should be abolished as ineffective and unneeded as a deterrent to major crime and as unwanted by a nation that champions the worth and dignity of the individual.

Conclusion

Slavery, atrocities, economic oppression, aggression and subversion are not solely the products of either Eastern or Western culture. They are products of lawlessness and man's inhumanity to man. Regardless of where they occur, they are crimes against all men, black and white, capitalist and Communist. As such they are properly the concern of all men.

For the people of the West, it is easy to overlook the truth connected with this philosophy although it is patently consistent with the Christian ethic. We are constantly made aware of the short-comings of the Communist and pro-Communist nations. Because of this and understanding pride, we tend to overlook the fact that the West has no grounds for complacency, self righteousness or smugness. Rather, we should have an abiding sense of debt to humanity coupled with a resolve to build with others an international society of law to secure to all men the blessings of liberty and justice. The fact that there is inhumanity practiced by men and governments is the compelling reason for—not against—a government of the whole.

The purpose here in pointing to the ugliness in Western culture is to show that while it may have produced the high point in the evolution of man as a social creature, bringing him his present high degree of freedom and dignity; it has also produced unparalleled barbarism and injustice. If we seek inhumanity among the Communist and non-Western nations surely we will find it but we can also find it in our own history. If we talk of unrest in the emergence of the Congo as being Communist-inspired, we must remember that the West is not without similar blame. Under the regime of Leopold of Belgium, it is believed that five to eight million Congolese lives were lost through torture and inhumane treatment. Hands and feet of African boys were cut off by Europeans and brought in by the basket-full—sometimes smoked for preservation—by overseers to garner favor with labor gang bosses. This form of punishment was a European innovation as mutilation was unknown to the Congolese.

The conclusion is inescapable that no culture has exclusive possession of the truth. It is also inescapable that deprivations of freedom and abridgments of dignity by governments, directly or indirectly, are no less wrong because they occur in NATO or other countries associated with Western culture.

Russians believe they have never had it so good and quite possibly this is correct. Certainly it is apparent that they are moving steadily in the direction of more liberty for the individual. In the United States personal liberty has reached a point as yet unmatched in any Communist nation, but the United States has much to learn in its quest for equality of opportunity for its Negro population. With some notable exceptions, progress is being made all around the world in securing freedom and dignity for man. These strides must continue and become more universal.

As the right to life is the first unalienable right without which other rights are useless, it is manifest that the future progress of man toward freedom must be made within a framework of peace. World peace cannot be justly imposed by a single nation of either the East or the West. A government of NATO countries would be justified only in the event Communist and neutral nations refused to join as equal members. Such a government formed without the participation of the Communist and neutral nations should make it abundantly clear that Communist and neutral participation and full membership by all nations would be welcome. Any other course would tend to widen the schism between East and West, lending support to the fears and claims of nations outside the covenant that it was an entity to promote the cold war and was in fact a military array of non-Communist nations with aggressive intent. This would lead to a more strongly solidified anti-Western Communist combination with the result that the world would be in a greater danger than is now the case.

From the outset, the movement to international government should be with universal intent. There is nothing so precious about Western culture that we should be unwilling to share its uplifting aspects, nor is there danger of loss of liberty from dealing with Communist and socialist nations so great that we should continue to avoid the path to freedom and dignity for all men which government of the whole affords. The way lies through representative government wherein the rights of the individual can be protected by law. Anything less than dedication to universal government lacks consistency with our stated belief in democracy and with our Christian heritage that all men are the creatures of God and created with certain unalienable rights, and that it is through government that these rights are secured.

World government is not only the challenge of the age, it is man's hope for a future in which men everywhere can breath clean air and walk above ground in freedom. Our motivation should not be fear of what could happen, but a realization of the rightness of what must happen. Individually and collectively we must get on with this most important task of learning to live together. The alternative is all to clear; but, again, the motivation should not be fear of death or destruction. The impetus for the establishment of a governed world should be the desire to move mankind to a higher pinnacle of justice and understanding from which he can more clearly see and serve his spiritual and physical self and by so doing serve his innermost faith.

"Give me a place to stand and I will move the world."

   —ARCHIMEDES, announcing
    the principle of the
    lever

INDIVIDUAL ACTION FOR PEACE

Non-military men like Gandhi who helped to free India in the face of the power of the British Empire, Frank C. Laubach who helped more than 60 million people learn to read, the world-renowned Albert Schweitzer of Lambarene in West Central Africa, have been inspirations for men everywhere.

These are examples of individuals working in different ways, but nevertheless working to alleviate, not compound, man's suffering. Consistently these men did not feel a void in their lives that had to be filled by participation in the destructive side of life; their activities and philosophies were as consistently constructive as possible, never equating militarism with goodness, patriotism or service to mankind.

It is submitted that people who lead such lives are really the substantial people in man's history. It is these people, together with men who lack their fame but share their spirit of good will and purpose, that should be the objects of man's admiration. Military leaders are more to be pitied than envied in the never-ceasing struggle to elevate man as a moral being.

But what of unspectacular efforts for peace? What can the individual do who is not a Schweitzer, Laubach

or a Gandhi, but who is nevertheless a person of good will
and of peace? There is a poem that goes:

> I am only one.
> But, I am one.
> I cannot do everything.
> But, I can do something.
> What I can do I ought to do.
> And what I ought to do
> I will do.

This poem of unknown authorship carries a simple,
but very cogent message. No citizen of a democracy
should ever feel that he cannot be an effective worker for
world peace. To fail to realize that there is much each of
us can do is to forfeit by default the freedom of action
attendant to democratic citizenship. It is not a question of
"Can I" be effective in the movement for world order and
peace, but rather "Will I."

The first requisite of effective action for peace is an
ingrained conviction that war and mass killing and even
the preparation for this barbarism is man's most immoral
activity. There must be embedded in one's philosophy
the firm belief that the marshalling of national resources
with the purposeful intent of destroying other peoples
and nations is organized mass immorality of the highest
magnitude. Freedom being essentially an individual matter, there must be the personal view that dedication to
militarism is the antithesis of freedom, and that no man
can be free and be bound to a war machine no matter how
many material advantages such bondage may bring to him
either directly or indirectly.

Service for peace is a way of life. Effective service
in this regard is a constant, not a mantle or a philosophy
to be used for economic gain or social acclaim. The peace-

maker as distinguished from the military man is dedicated to a way of life, not death.

Only relatively few of the millions of Americans who desire world peace belong to peace organizations or have anything to do with them. The informative materials published by peace groups are generally read only by a handful of people. Radio and television programs when sponsored by peace groups do not invoke great waves of public enthusiasm. These are some of the conclusions reached after a careful study of the reticence of Americans to work for world peace.[1]

It is concluded that this failure to join actively in peace efforts is not entirely the fault of the people, but is in part attributable to the fact that the masses have been conditioned to react to certain techniques of selling that have not been employed by peace organizations.

The success of a national periodical is gauged by the number of millions of readers it attracts. On the other hand, a peace publication would be a phenomenal success if a circulation of 100,000 could be attained. The well-known popular magazines read by millions meet the double test of interest and understandability. To hold the interest of Americans, future peace publications must have these two characteristics, delivering their message in interesting and understandable fashion. This can be a significant contribution by those involved in the editing and publishing of peace materials.

A major circulation difficulty with peace publications is that they recommend change and because of this they are controversial. They are, therefore, instinctively read with some mistrust by all but the dedicated inner circle of adherents. But we are faced with the fact that change

1. Publication by the Institute for International Order entitled *Action for Peace* July, 1959.

is desperately needed, that publications in the field of world peace are in turn needed. There should be a constant effort by individuals who produce these materials to see that the publications issued by peace organizations are made more understandable and interesting. They should address the contents of these publications to the more than 70 per cent of the American public who presently support the United Nations. As individuals determine the actions and policies of peace organizations, persons in a position of leadership within these groups must exercise their influence to the end that peace publications become more effective. Interest can be enhanced by relating the printed material to current events; arguments for world law and added strength for the United Nations should be related to current, local and world problems.

People are cautious and hesitant to entertain ideas that are controversial, and peace groups are controversial because they fly in the face of the ingrained militarism in our society. This is an extraordinary and inhibiting factor that works against mass acceptance of the basic ideas and programs that would change our military way of life. But not all of militarism is attractive, and concentration should be made by peace groups and outspoken individuals on those many unpalatable facets of the war program. While militarism is good for business and while it brings to many economic advantage, the deprivation of freedoms, the loss of sovereignty, the base immorality should be the objects of concentrated attention.

It is the individual that is the key to world peace. Yet, he so often fails to realize this. Each individual citizen, earnestly striving to be effective in the movement for world law, can make a significant contribution by his activity. His significance is enhanced by working with others in organizations dedicated to the creation of better world understanding.

In specific terms, just what are these things that an individual can do working alone and with others? It is well, then, to ennumerate some of the activities that have been successfully carried out in the past by individuals working singly and together. Appendix C of this volume contains a listing of practical actions that are available to all individuals wishing to become effective in the movement for world peace through law. It should be emphasized that peace activities should not be confined to United Nations Week. Assisting in the field of world understanding is in large measure a way of life that should pervade our thinking and actions throughout the year.

"I believe that we must come to realize that we are irreversibly part of a world wide human community, but that it is not a community that enjoys the structure of safeguards of a civilized society. At home we live under law. We play our part in promoting the general welfare. We share some sense of national purpose. These are surely the minimum conditions of a truly civic life, or a life in society that deserves the name of human. . . . But all are lacking in our international world. The introductions of such fundamental institutions should be the first aim of our world policy."

—ADLAI STEVENSON

THE PHILOSOPHY OF PEACE

The tragic death of President Kennedy late in 1963 had greater pathos because his youth, his wife—possibly our finest first lady—his young children, his creation of the Peace Corps and his efforts on behalf of civil rights, had identified him personally to many Americans.

A line of people six abreast—the line at times six to ten miles long—moved past the President's bier as he lay in state in the rotunda of the Capitol. The procession continued throughout a day and night in sub-freezing weather. After the President was buried in Arlington, hundreds of thousands of Americans visited his grave within a few days after his interment in the city of the dead across the Potomac River from Washington.

For several days immediately following the assassination of President Kennedy, radio and television stations carried nothing but commentaries concerning the events surrounding the death of the President. The press coverage of the assassination was of equal thoroughness. Never before has the death of one man received such simultaneous emphasis. The general concern for this man's death swept the world and the feelings of most Americans were severely wrenched by this loss to our nation.

The general feeling was one of disbelief. As the truth of the assassination came with its full force upon the conscience of the citizenry, some tried to place the blame for the killing on the city of Dallas where it occurred. Others sought to find a flaw in the nation's structure that could have brought on the tragedy. The right wing blamed the Communists, the left wing blamed the hate groups of the conservatives, and the moderates blamed the extremists on both sides. The reaction of most Americans was to point the finger of accusation at some single segment or division of our society and to fail to appraise the over-all moral position of the nation relative to its concern for mankind.

The overriding flaw in the life of our nation escaped those participating in this appraisal of our national life. It probably failed to register on any of those who trudged past the 122,000 white markers in Arlington Cemetery to view the final resting place of the President. It likely did not occur to the millions here and abroad who viewed and read the details of the last rites for President Kennedy.

Yet, what of those thousands of other young men who, like the young President, lie in Arlington? What of the millions of young men now living who are presently threatened with death by nuclear blast and radiation? What of our nation's drive to develop more deadly weapons of death whose effectiveness is measured in megakills —the number of millions of people they will kill? What of the more than fifty billion dollars we spend annually for the maintenance of a military machine which threatens the existence of our very species? Again, part of the pathos connected with the death of the young President lay in the fact that he was the father of young children, but where is our concern for the millions of young children throughout the world who are threatened by the devices of death set and primed in the planes, submarines and missile silos of America and the other nuclear powers? Where is our concern for mankind generally?

The immediate reaction of most people to the news that the President of the United States had been assassinated was: "I can't believe it." This reaction revealed an inability to grasp fully the enormity of the tragedy.[1] This was a most human reaction. We simply do not, for the sake of our sanity, let our thoughts dwell long on the possible horrors that might befall us. Therefore, when we are confronted with a deep tragedy we are generally not prepared. The more horrible the event, the less prepared we are to accept it. Our preparedness is even less if such an event has not occurred in recent times or has never confronted us before.

So it is with the threat to nations of nuclear destruction. All scientific evidence indicates that it can happen. Government leaders in Russia and America say that they would use nuclear bombs under certain circumstances. But could nuclear holocaust really happen here? We remember vaguely the destruction of Nagasaki and Hiroshima; these were but other cities like Coventry and Rotterdam that were bombed during World War II. No entire nation has ever been wiped out, nor a whole people destroyed. Surely, no major power would now directly and intentionally start a war with another major power because of the certain retaliatory devastation that she would suffer. Possibly so. But what of an untoward event or warped personality? It was such an event and personality that caused the tragic death of our President in Dallas. The nation survived—and there was no real question but that it would—because the founders of our republic made provisions for such a contingency. The na-

1. See: editorial by Norman Cousins in the December 21, 1963, issue of the *Saturday Review* entitled, "Can Civilization Be Assassinated?"

tion survived because there had been those wise enough to see the possibility of the event and make provision for it.

People generally must now ask the question what will happen to mankind should some untoward event or warped personality trigger the weapons of annihilation now aimed at the heartlands of the great powers? If some survive but millions perish, would this make the deed any the less tragic or less morally wrong? Shall we not act to prevent such desecration to God's handiwork now?

The fact is that both America and Russia now place in the hands of numerous individuals nuclear devices which could start a chain reaction that could destroy entire nations, their peoples and even our species. The major powers will soon be joined by other powers possessing the same potential for destruction, such potential being, in turn, placed in the hands of additional numbers of individuals subject to human mistakes and failings.

Submarines of both America and Russia now ply the seas equipped with nuclear warhead-carrying missiles. Every city in both nations is within the range of these missiles. Each submarine captain has the capacity to launch one or more of these devices. In addition, the United States has hundreds of jet planes in the air twenty-four hours a day close to the Soviet Union. Each plane is fully loaded with hydrogen explosives.

Certainly great precaution is taken to insure that irresponsible action will not occur, but orders are transmitted and action taken by individuals. Human beings make errors and are subject to many variations in human personality, motivation and behavior. These men with the power to kill millions are no doubt carefully screened, but no psychologist or other evaluator can probe the innermost recesses of the mind of every man entrusted with nuclear devices to reveal what bitterness, resentment or

warped sense of patriotism or right and wrong may be
stored deep within. Changes in personality occur and no
one can determine precisely how an individual will react
to all of a limitless number of varying circumstances. An
individual plane, missile or submarine commander may
be motivated by what he feels to be his highest duty to
country in turning the weapons under his control against
his own or some other nation. A citizen of the United
States—a former United States Marine—shot and killed
the President of the United States. This seemed unbe-
lieveable, but it happened. The Secret Service could not
possibly have known the mind of every spectator along the
route the President took in Dallas. Similarly, it is impossible to know precisely the mind of every individual—
and the number continues to grow—who has the power to
annihilate millions of human beings.

It has been suggested that only the President can
authorize the use of nuclear weapons. If each officer in
control of nuclear weapons would first have to receive
arming information from the United States or Europe,
what would he do if Europe and the U. S. were "knocked
out" in the first wave of nuclear war?

Obviously, the entire theory of nuclear deterrence including the threat of massive retaliation hinges on the
ability of the nation first hit to retaliate with equal devastation. Clearly, outbound air and sea born naval commanders must have the power to proceed to destroy the
enemy if the horrendous policy of nuclear deterrence is
to have force and effect. Even if some method could be
devised to insure against the unintentional use of atomic
weapons, there is no assurance that other nuclear powers
will adopt our safety procedures. And, of course, we
would be slow to reveal such procedures to any but our
closest allies.

But suppose, in fact, that only the President can press the nuclear trigger. The duties of his office are tremendously taxing and it is certainly possible for a president to fall victim to human error and even mental derangement.

There can, then, be no such thing as a truly safe nuclear deterrent force. Inherent in the concept of nuclear deterrence is the fact that it is manmade and therefore subject to human error. If it ever becomes totally machine controlled it will then be subject to mechanical malfunction. For mankind to be safe from the likelihood of eventual nuclear disaster, nuclear deterrence must be replaced by a greater deterrent—that of universal arms control through law and government of the whole.

What can be done? We can through an ordered disarmament reduce the number of devices of mass destruction subject to use by mistake and by aberrant commanders; that is, in part, at least, disarm the potential mass assassin. Most important, and essential to a permanent secure peace and disarmament, we must cultivate a devotion, dedication, concern and patriotism for the whole of mankind which will find its expression in a world political authority; this authority to receive the individual citizen's first allegiance. The movement for such a world government must begin with the people themselves because national government leaders are so dedicated to the status quo that seemingly serves them well that they are unlikely to view the problem of mankind other than through nationalistic eyes—a "what's good for my country is good for the world" philosophy. International government can provide the framework—the object—for such individual concern for the whole of our human society. Within such a context of government the untoward event, the misdeeds of a military commander, miscalculations, mistakes and human error will not escalate into world-wide catastrophe for mankind. Our world must make provision for its orderly continuance should an untoward nuclear event occur. With a world government a nuclear accident would be far less likely as emphasis would shift from the preparation for war at the national level to the solution of the problems of everyday living at the world level. Then should a nuclear accident occur, it would not escalate into world-wide destruction, but be isolated and contained with minimal cost in human lives and property damage.

In reappraising our nation's moral posture and security, we must surely consider the threat from the very thing many now believe to be our salvation, that is, our military might. What does it matter if our nuclear devices are used deliberately or not if they cause the death of our nation? What does it matter to mankind what nation uses nuclear weapons first if millions of people are killed and nations destroyed? We must consider these questions as we appraise our nation's moral footing and position of security in the nuclear age.

It is difficult to understand how we as a nation can accommodate ourselves to a balance of terror, a period of non-violence which history tells us cannot be permanent and cannot work as a substitute for law and government in our quest for peace, freedom and justice. We have deluded ourselves into thinking that peace and justice with freedom can somehow be achieved and insured by threatening to annihilate those nations with whom we disagree. Our enemy in turn suffers from the same delusion and threatens to annihilate us. Both the United States and the Soviet Union are well able to carry out these reciprocal threats. Other nations will soon join these two major powers in this macabre display of disrespect for the worth of mankind. As a nation we devote great portions of our national energies to insure our ability to carry out our threat to destroy our enemy should he violate certain conditions which we—not a world governmental authority—have set forth. Our adversary also devotes his substance in large measure to the same inhuman business.

A person who had been a teenager in Nazi Germany during World War II found a picture of herself taken during those terrible years. She found the picture some twenty years after the war had ended and was amazed to see how happy she appeared in the picture. The picture showed her smiling brightly. In the photograph she was wearing a coat that had belonged to one of her friends who had been murdered by the Nazis only a short time before the picture was snapped. She remembers further that at the time the picture was taken her mother was about to be shipped away to a concentration camp. On finding the picture after the war, she asked herself how could she have possibly been so happy under such circumstances? The answer, she says, is simple; she had no basis for comparing the Nazi government and its actions to any other governmental system. The Nazi government is all she had ever known. Because her government said it was necessary to deport Jews, loyalty to country—patriotism—made objection seem wrong. The acts of her government seemed to be simply in the scheme of things, and they were accepted as necessary without moral judgment by the citizenry. Air raids were of immediate concern; life seemed fleeting, and the emphasis was to live for the moment. She recalls a feeling of contentment under Nazism. An air raid free night, an extra ration of food, a friendly act, a bar of soap—little things—meant happiness. Concern was for the immediate. She was happy when her mother was sent to a concentration camp because her mother would be free from the almost nightly air raids. It was only after the war—after the crimes of her government had been committed—that she realized the moral turpitude of the acts of the Nazi regime.[2]

There is a definite parallel between the apathy of some German citizens who knew of Nazi barbarisms during World War II and our moral position today as we tolerate and nurture our military machines of mass murder, threaten to destroy other nations and their people, fail to seek with all our energies equity, liberty, security and peace for all mankind within a framework of world law and government.

2. See: article by Margret Hofmann entitled "What We Don't Know" in the December 21, 1963, issue of the *Saturday Review*.

"... government on a worldwide scale has now become one of the necessary conditions for the survival of mankind. The hope for a world government ought therefore now to take a high place in our inventory of human hopes."

—Arnold Toynbee

THE LARGE VIEW

In order to gain an objective perspective of world affairs, it is necessary for an individual to see his country as one among many of equal dignity rather than viewing his particular nation as the epicenter of the universe. No single nation can be deemed indisputably correct with truth exclusively on its side. We must consider the overall world picture, seeing events and conditions as they affect all people and all nations. Failing to do this leads to rationalizations which in the past have justified world wars. For example, the Germans justified their invasion of Russia by saying that intelligence reports made it obvious that Soviet Russia was using the Russo-German Pact merely to gain time and that Russia was secretly arming to the utmost of her ability ultimately to attack Germany. Viewed in this light, Germany reasoned that she could not continue to expose herself to such mortal danger. To forestall this "Bolshevik treachery," the Fuhrer attacked Russia in "self defense" to prevent aggression by the Red Army which was characterized to Germans as the greatest threat ever posed to European civilization.

Taken from any particular nation's point of view, conclusions as to international right and wrong are indisputable, unchallengeable and absolute to the citizenry of that particular country. But it is patently clear that all citizens in all countries cannot be absolutely right, and just as surely all national points of view cannot be correct as they will inevitably diverge so greatly. A picture of world affairs gained strictly from the point of view of one nation can have but little if any relation to objective appraisal and truth because the process used disavows objectivity.

To arrive at a more orderly relationship among nations, we must try to arrive at a more objective method of observing and judging world affairs. Without such an approach to world difficulties, we will never perceive the true problems that stand athwart man's pathway to world peace.

In the second century A.D. in Alexandria, Ptolemy explained that the world was the center of the universe, that the sun, moon and all stars revolved about the earth. This theory was unchallenged for fourteen hundred years. Thus, under the systems of observation used at that time the geocentric system was satisfying and worked perfectly. It, for example, fitted very nicely the story of the creation of the universe as told in the Bible, and it became a doctrine approved by the Church. However, later using new methods of observation, Copernicus brought man closer to the truth and set forth the proposition that the earth itself rotated and, like other planets in space, it revolved about the sun. The observations of Copernicus were later reinforced by the work of Kepler and Galileo, but these new ideas were condemned by church authorities as heresy and rejected by some of the greatest astronomers and scientists of that day.

Similarly, it is important for us today not to consider our country as the epicenter of the world about which other nations move. World problems must be viewed in proper perspective and in context with the realization that there is a political universe. It is folly to feel that we can settle world problems by viewing them strictly as they relate to our own nation. It is important to remember that it is not the problems of the world that are insoluble; our difficulty lies in the fact that we seek their solution through provincial concepts. We fail to take the world-wide view of world problems. We tend to see them only from the point of view of our particular nation and not from the point of view of the needs of all mankind. We must rise above the dogma of this nation-centric concept and realize that to solve the problem of recurring international warfare and in particular to contain the competition between the major powers we must move towards a governed world; and, in this movement, it is vital to its success to appraise international problems from an international point of view.

The founders of modern political democracy understood that freedom in human society is relative, and that freedom in its absolute sense is bound to lead to anarchy and then to violence, which was the exact opposite from the ordered society they sought to create. They realized that freedom is secured by limiting the free exercise of human impulses through generally applied compulsions or laws. It is apparent that freedom can be granted to an individual only to the extent that his freedom does not unreasonably impinge on the freedom of his neighbor. It is patently clear that a laissez faire economy never existed in its pure form because it lacked the restraints and compulsions necessary to an ordered economy. As power is gained by the few they find themselves in a position to take advantage of the less powerful. Thus, unbridled freedom in the hands of the powerful clearly leaves opportunity for exploitation. Compulsions in the form of laws are necessary to curb unrestrained actions by those who would take advantage of their positions of power. Absolute free enterprise would breed monopoly which would be the antithesis of free enterprise. A totally free enterprise system would be self-destructive.

Attempts at relatively free enterprise in America and in England brought two or three decades of industrialization which, while it created undreamed of wealth, at the same time created previously unknown human misery, frustration and dependency, the reverse of freedom. Bitter resentment by the millions who had lost their independence and freedom and whose talents had been exploited by the more powerful sought relief, and such creations as modern socialism, trade unionism, labor legislation, social security, inheritance taxation and other devices were born to try to overcome injustices that had arisen from the attempt to create absolute economic freedom. Loss of human freedom was the price of our attempt to create absolute economic freedom. It became apparent that compulsions in the form of laws were essential to a smooth functioning economy wherein individuals enjoy maximum freedom. Restraints on the individual are absolutely essential to his freedom and he must come to realize that restraints on his nation are just as essential to freedom.

Individual nations fearing attack from without, and seeking self-sufficiency, resort to more social and economic planning which results in the transfer of more and more authority by individuals to the national government. As a nation strives for security, it finds itself in absolute opposition to free enterprise. But this is justified under the term "national security." High tariffs, subsidies, manipulations and artificial stimulation of the economy through

government financing completely distorts the economic
picture and robs individuals of their maximum freedom.

Freedom in the human sense is diametrically opposite
from freedom among animals. For example, the tiger and
the shark are free to destroy. Human freedom is freedom
from being destroyed, oppressed or exploited. It means
protection from innumerable dangers; it means the right
to be allowed to pursue one's calling reasonably un-
restricted. History had demonstrated that law is the one
method that gains for man his largest measure of individual protection and freedom. Human freedom can exist
only within a framework of law. The fact that Russia is
Communist and that the United States is capitalist is not
the reason for antagonisms between these countries. Varying economic systems are not the reason behind international warfare. For example, England and Germany
were both capitalist countries but have opposed each other
in two world wars. International warfare is the product
of a system which we have tolerated wherein ungoverned
nations are given more and more power by their citizens
in the name of national security. Competition between the
major powers leads to more and more concentration of
authority in national governments which, in turn, leads to
over-protection and to the limitation of individual freedom. The process tends toward totalitarianism and repeated clashes between competing national units. No
major power dares cease its armament production; in its
frenzy to keep militarily ahead of its competition, it taxes
and restrains individual freedom. These restraints continue
to mount as each major power proceeds in the direction of
becoming an arsenal state. Ironically, individual freedom
sacrificed in the name of national security has purchased no
security, but rather armaments with which the citizens of

the major powers will eventually destroy each other in the absence of a governed world.

The wholesale killing in international warfare during the twentieth century has shown the inability of Christianity and the other major religions to prevent world wars in modern times. To the civilizing influences of religion in the world must be added a form of legal order to impose upon man certain principles of human conduct. Too often the church has capitulated and abandoned itself to the base instincts of man when national and sectional policy has been deemed religious policy. The injunction that "thou shall not kill" loses its moral suasion if it comes to mean that thou shall not kill one's own countrymen but that it is a virtue to kill the citizens of an enemy nation. The concepts of universalism and oneness and of a supreme creator and law-giver can greatly assist man in his quest for world order. Conversely, an ordered world under law wherein man's base drives are contained and international warfare eliminated would be spiritually purifying for man universally. Through world government man can purge himself of the diabolical nationalistic drive that now compels him to prepare for the annihilation of his brother.

We now feel that the nation is the highest level of social order. This concept is tending to push capitalist and Communist nations toward an all out effort on the part of each to become militarily the most powerful. In this effort initial goals and principles of each country tend to become subverted as sovereign states in competition with one another for power become more and more totalitarian.

The relationship between the commoner and the feudal landlords of the Middle Ages was similar to that which exist today between nation-states and their citizens. Frequently the commoner was called upon to take up arms to fight neighboring barons and landlords in order to protect the sovereignty of their own baron or landlord. Each little kingdom looked upon the power and influence of the adjoining kingdom with fear and distrust. Security was obtained by attacking another's domain and eliminating the threat to the feudal estate. There was constant quarreling among barons and feudal landlords. As a result combinations for security became larger; kingdoms grew as the people gravitated to the more popular kings. Medieval history illustrates that there is a fundamental instinct for man to combine with other men to seek freedom and security. The search for freedom and security through combination led to the development of the nation-state which served man well until increasing technological, scientific and economic developments created interdependence and competition between nations. Presently we are at the same stage of social evolution in which man found himself in the thirteenth century; far from enjoying freedom, we have moved into a state of multiplicity of conflicting sovereign nations which as they continue to expand in their military commitment and as they place more restrictions on individual freedoms, deprive man of his freedom, protection and security which was originally promised him by the individual nation-state.

The military commitment of the modern nation-state increasingly and ironically deprives man of those freedoms he seeks to secure. Feudalism created serfdom because the competition between the landlords and land barons led to debilitating wars, destruction, starvation and ultimately to the destruction of the system itself. Nations in effect have now taken the place of barons and counts of old.

Individuals increasingly have their liberties circumscribed by their national governments in the name of "national security." The identification of the interests of a king with his people led to despotism, and today we have much the same thing as we identify national interests with individual interests. We now have a system of national feudalism which will continue to drain us of our liberty and will eventually destroy us unless we recognize man's basic oneness and in that spirit create an international political entity to bring freedom to all men and to protect ourselves and our posterity from nuclear destruction.

It is argued that war is in the nature of man. Even if this is true, there are many things—among them smallpox, yellow fever, and polio—also a part of human experience, which man has learned to control. Thus, it could be with war. We must look to the causes of war and treat this bent in man's nature effectively—if in fact it is a part of his nature—so that periodically millions of people do not die from it. Daily in our individual towns we see proof of the fact that through government man's baseness can be contained. None of us would vote to eliminate all government from our town, state or nation, yet we continue to seek world order by every conceivable method short of government. There can be no substitute for government if we want to preserve our nations and their peoples and secure our maximum freedom.

The lack of a superior sovereignty caused feudal landlords and now nation-states to engage in war. Throughout history there has been an evolving tendency for man to move his political allegiance from one social unit to a larger social unit. As a superior sovereignty was acknowledged these units tended to become quiescent and people once hostile began living together and working together in peace and freedom.

In our modern world, on the surface of things, it would appear that large armies protect one's country and that in order to be free from attack a superior armed force should be maintained. But every nation cannot be superior in armed might and the competition between the major powers has brought us to the point in history where any one of several nations not only has the power but the willingness to set in motion forces that could destroy all human life. This crystalizes the present danger to man of the uncontrolled nation-state. Each of the major powers including the United States constitutes a threat to mankind. The threat of the imposition of an alien ideology pales into insignificance when compared to the modern fact of life that we as individuals regardless of where we live are constantly threatened with the destruction of our lives and property by the uncontrolled militarism of the major powers.

We are conducting our national affairs under the fallacious premise that military power will protect our country. However, the United States, the Soviet Union, Belgium, Czechoslovakia and Yugoslavia were among the nations that practiced militarism and universal conscription before World War II, but these practices did not save our nations from the horrors of that conflict. On the other hand, after World War I, restriction on the tonnage of battleships, reduction in the caliber of guns, prohibition of submarines and gas warfare did not prevent World War II.

Neither armament nor disarmament constitutes a cure for the problem of international warfare, but of the two our present approach through massive armaments is the more dangerous because the resulting destruction from another war will be the greater. There is no practical substitute in modern times for an integration of conflicting national sovereignties into a unified and higher sovereignty capable of enhancing a legal structure wherein people can enjoy equal security and freedom under law.

The great democratic ideals of the eighteenth century were served well by the nation-state for a hundred years, but increasing international contact now required these ideals to be elevated to the international level of man's society. The philosophy that the state is the absolute sovereign has become a monstrous totalitarian concept, which carries with it the essence of Fascism. While the United States, Great Britian, France and the Soviet Union were created to secure freedom and liberty to their people, it is no longer possible for these nations to prevent war. Millions of their citizens have died and billions of their dollars have been wasted for the preservation not of liberty but of the nation-state. Had liberty and freedom been the goal we could not have settled for less than law and order. For decades now the nation-state has ceased to serve as an institution capable of protecting its citizens from war. We are now faced not with surrendering national sovereignty but of regaining it through the creation of an international political organization which we lack and so critically need. The point cannot be too strongly emphasized that governments are created to serve people and not people to serve governments. In our failure to move in the direction of world government we have agreed to serve the tyranny of the nation-state and have prostrated ourselves before the nation-state as though it and not man was of supreme worth. A continuation of this idolatry will lead to a destruction not only of the idol, but of man himself.

Certainly the modern nation-state is not providing for individual freedom if every twenty years our families are torn apart, our young people are killed and our earnings regularly taken from us in confiscatory taxation to be used for the purchase of armaments. The great threat to individual liberty is the growing power of the nation-state as it seeks the impossible—peace and security through armament.

Internationalism can be distinguished from universalism. The first, second, and third communist internationals were in reality means of forging a strong bond between separate states of like political persuasion. Similarly, NATO is a military alliance between nations who fear the Soviet Union or who claim such fear in order to gain economic advantages. With such alliance economic restrictions are relaxed but restrictions on outside nations are tightened. Together with the Warsaw Pact these alliances could be denominated as international, but very clearly they are not universal and were not so intended. These international but not universal alliances claim to be instruments of international peace whereas in reality they are military and economic combinations which lack the universal political authority essential to the elimination of international war.

Under the Covenant of the League of Nations, peace was to be maintained by meetings and discussions between sovereign nations. Effective sanctions could be levied only when there was unanimity and any national government could withdraw from the League at will. The League did excellent work in settling conflicts between small nations, but was unable to effect settlements between the major powers. When Japan, Germany and Italy withdrew from the League, it became apparent that it had suffered a mortal blow. A truly international authority with sufficient power could have opposed Hitler when he repudiated the Locarno Pact and occupied the Rhineland and when Italy launched aggression in Ethiopia. The League of Nations failed because it was founded on the false premise that peace can be established by bringing national units together in discussion and debate without making provision for controlling their aggressive activities.

The significant World War II agreements were: The Atlantic Charter, the United Nations Declaration, the Moscow Agreements, the Dumbarton Oaks Proposal, the Teheran and Yalta Communiques and the San Francisco Charter. These all emphasized that the things to be done would be done between sovereign nations. The fault in these arrangements lay in the fact that the problem of international warfare is a problem of mankind and between all peoples and not a problem of nations.

It is universalism and not internationalism that should receive our emphasis.

National self-determination is now an anachronism because it claims for every nation the right to do as it pleases within its own frontier regardless of how vicious or detrimental its actions might be to the rest of the world. We must detach ourselves from the eighteenth-century idea of unfettered nationalism. How the men of one nation are treated is the business of all men. While maintaining the fiction of independence, nations today often have to act because of actions taken within another nation over which the reacting nation has no control. The Declaration of War by the Congress after the Japanese attack on Pearl Harbor was certainly not a sovereign act as it was made necessary by decisions rendered by the Imperial War Council in Tokyo, much as war was forced on the Soviet Union by decisions made in Berlin.

Modern nationalism is defended on the basis that liberty reposes in the nation-state. The fact is that liberty reposes in the individual and not in the nation-state. The nation-state was designed to insure man's liberty and it served this function until modern technological advancements brought nations so close together that they became competing units, fiercely rivaling each other as did the city-states of old. Now without a super sovereignty this competition is increasingly stripping man of his freedom and constitutes his greatest threat. It is essential that there be regulation of the interrelations of self-determined sovereign units. The hallmark of independence and self-determination is the ability to guarantee freedom against aggression and destruction from without and to guarantee maximum freedom within. Obviously the major powers today lack this ability; we are led from one cataclysmic political precipice to another, as our individual liberties become more and more restricted and our earnings siphoned away by exorbitant taxation.

The unlimited sovereignty of the modern nation-state has become license to do unlimited mischief. Human rights must now be elevated to take their rightful place as superior to national rights. Regard for individual freedom must become superior to worship of the nation-state. We have failed to recognize that a peaceful international society can not exist without our dedication to the preservation of the rights of its members. In making an idol of the nation-state, we are losing our individual freedoms and degrading ourselves morally in the bargain. Universal sovereignty is essential to universal peace. International war is built into our present international system of separate national sovereign units, each having no higher allegiance than itself, each acting without juridical restraint. While the present system permits collective security against small nations, regional arrangements are ineffective to prevent an eventual conflict between the major powers. There is extant the international political hypocrisy that if a small nation commits an immoral act it will be punished, but if a major power commits an immoral act it will not feel the sting of international sanctions and punishment. The unfathomable and unanswerable question of modern time is why we so steadfastly avoid the realization that international law and government are essential to international peace and to the preservation of our nation and its institutions.

The Poles, Russians, Hungarians, Rumanians, Serbs and Bulgars have distrusted one another and fought wars in Europe for centuries, but these very same people settling in the United States of America ceased fighting, became completely amiable, and now live and work together without waging war. This is so because they found a common bond in a common sovereignty. Similarly, Frenchmen, Italians and Germans live in peace in Switzerland. There is not the slightest doubt that this same living together of people of various backgrounds in peace could be effected on a world-wide basis as between all men through the creation of an effective democratic international political institution of law and government to speak and act for all mankind. The creation of this institution constitutes the primary imperative of the nuclear age.

The present idle drift toward an effective international political organization must be replaced with concerted effort and planning lest in our aimlessness nations and mankind slip over the brink into a war of annihilation.

The Cuban crisis in October of 1962 well illustrated the fact that the fate of mankind now lies in the hands of a few heads of state who settle their major differences by the threat of nuclear war. This world oligarchy must be replaced by a democratic political institution of the whole wherein government and courts of law replace the whim and caprice of heads of state in the settlement of international differences.

The danger to his species, the loss of freedoms and the gross immorality of the present war system is not a fact that the mind of man can any longer accept with equanimity.

Can we avoid a nuclear war of annihilation? The answer lies with the people of the world. Individual citizens must become involved in the quest to substitute law for the present war system among nations.

It is a time to place emphasis on the common needs and fundamental similarities of the peoples of all nations. It is clearly a time for individual action to achieve world peace through world law in the nuclear age.

PART

V | APPENDIXES

APPENDIX A

UNIVERSAL DECLARATION OF HUMAN RIGHTS

Preamble

Whereas recognition of the inherent dignity and of the equal and inalienable rights of all members of the human family is the foundation of freedom, justice and peace in the world,

Whereas disregard and contempt for human rights have resulted in barbarous acts which have outraged the conscience of mankind, and the advent of a world in which human beings shall enjoy freedom of speech and belief and freedom from fear and want has been proclaimed as the highest aspirations of the common people,

Whereas it is essential, if man is not to be compelled to have recourse, as a last resort, to rebellion against tyranny and oppression, that human rights should be protected by the rule of law,

Whereas it is essential to promote the development of friendly relations between nations,

Whereas the peoples of the United Nations have in the Charter reaffirmed their faith in fundamental human rights, in the dignity and worth of the human person and in the equal rights of men and women and have determined to promote social progress and better standards of life in larger freedom,

Whereas Member States have pledged themselves to achieve, in cooperation with the United Nations, the promotion of universal respect for and observance of human rights and fundamental freedoms,

Whereas a common understanding of these rights and freedoms is of the greatest importance for the full realization of this pledge,

NOW THEREFORE
THE GENERAL ASSEMBLY proclaims

This UNIVERSAL DECLARATION OF HUMAN RIGHTS as a common standard of achievement for all peoples and all nations, to the end that every individual and every organ of society, keeping this Declaration constantly in mind, shall strive by teaching and education to promote respect for these rights and freedoms and by progressive measures, national and international, to secure their universal and effective recognition and observance, both among the peoples of Member States themselves and among the peoples of territories under their jurisdiction.

Article 1: All human beings are born free and equal in dignity and rights. They are endowed with reason and conscience and should act towards one another in a spirit of brotherhood.

Article 2: Everyone is entitled to all the rights and freedoms set forth in this Declaration, without distinction of any kind, such as race, color, sex, language, religion, political or other opinion, national or social origin, property, birth or other status. Furthermore, no distinction shall be made on the basis of the political, jurisdictional or international status of the country or territory to which a person belongs, whether it be independent, trust, nonself-governing or under any other limitation of sovereignty.

Article 3: Everyone has the right to life, liberty and security of person.

Article 4: No one shall be held in slavery or servitude; slavery and the slave trade shall be prohibited in all their forms.

Article 5: No one shall be subjected to torture or to cruel, inhuman or degrading treatment or punishment.

Article 6: Everyone has the right to recognition everywhere as a person before the law.

Article 7: All are equal before the law and are entitled without any discrimination to equal protection of the law. All are entitled to equal protection against any discrimination in violation of this Declaration and against any incitement to such discrimination.

Article 8: Everyone has the right to an effective remedy by the competent national tribunals for acts violating the fundamental rights granted him by the constitution or by law.

Article 9: No one shall be subjected to arbitrary arrest, detention or exile.

Article 10: Everyone is entitled in full equality to a fair and public hearing by an independent and impartial tribunal, in the determination of his rights and obligations and of any criminal charge against him.

Article 11: (1) Everyone charged with a penal offence has the right to be presumed innocent until proved guilty according to law in a public trial at which he has had all the guarantees necessary for his defense.

(2) No one shall be held guilty of any penal offence on account of any act or omission which did not constitute a penal offence, under national or international law, at the time when it was committed. Nor shall a

heavier penalty be imposed than the one that was applicable at the time the penal offence was committed.

Article 12: No one shall be subjected to arbitrary interference with his privacy, family, home or correspondence, nor to attacks upon his honor and reputation. Everyone has the right to the protection of the law against such interference or attacks.

Article 13: (1) Everyone has the right to freedom of movement and residence within the borders of each state.

(2) Everyone has the right to leave any country, including his own, and to return to his country.

Article 14: (1) Everyone has the right to seek and to enjoy in other countries asylum from persecution.

(2) This right may not be invoked in the case of prosecutions genuinely arising from non-political crimes or from acts contrary to the purposes and principles of the United Nations.

Article 15: (1) Everyone has the right to a nationality.

(2) No one shall be arbitrarily deprived of his nationality nor denied the right to change his nationality.

Article 16: (1) Men and women of full age, without any limitations due to race, nationality or religion, have the right to marry and to found a family. They are entitled to equal rights as to marriage, during marriage and at its dissolution.

(2) Marriage shall be entered into only with the free and full consent of the intending spouses.

(3) The family is the natural and fundamental group unit of society and is entitled to protection by society and the State.

Article 17: (1) Everyone has the right to own property alone as well as in association with others.

(2) No one shall be arbitrarily deprived of his property.

Article 18: Everyone has the right to freedom of thought, conscience and religion; this right includes freedom to change his religion or belief, and freedom, either alone or in community with others and in public or private, to manifest his religion or belief in teaching, practice, worship and observance.

Article 19: Everyone has the right to freedom of opinion and expression; this right includes freedom to hold opinions without interference and to seek, receive and impart information and ideas through any media and regardless of frontiers.

Article 20: (1) Everyone has the right to freedom of peaceful assembly and association.

(2) No one may be compelled to belong to an association.

Article 21: (1) Everyone has the right to take part in the government of his country, directly or through freely chosen representatives.

(2) Everyone has the right of equal access to public service in his country.

(3) The will of the people shall be the basis of the authority of government; this will shall be expressed in periodic and genuine elections which shall be by universal and equal suffrage and shall be held by secret vote or by equivalent free voting procedures.

Article 22: Everyone, as a member of society, has the right to social security and is entitled to realization, through national effort and international co-operation and in accordance with the organization and resources of each state, of the economic, social and cultural rights indispensable for his dignity and the free development of his personality.

Article 23: (1) Everyone has the right to work, to free choice of employment, to just and favorable conditions of work and to protection against unemployment.

(2) Everyone, without any discrimination, has the right to equal pay for equal work.

(3) Everyone who works has the right to just and favorable remuneration insuring for himself and his family an existence worthy of human dignity, and supplemented, if necessary, by other means of social protection.

(4) Everyone has the right to form and to join trade unions for the protection of his interests.

Article 24: Everyone has the right to rest and leisure, including reasonable limitation of working hours and periodic holidays with pay.

Article 25: (1) Everyone has the right to a standard of living adequate for the health and well-being of himself and of his family, including food, clothing, housing, and medical care and necessary social service, and the right to security in the event of unemployment, sickness, disability, widowhood, old age or other lack of livelihood in circumstances beyond his control.

(2) Motherhood and childhood are entitled to special care and assistance. All children, whether born in or out of wedlock, shall enjoy the same social protection.

Article 26: (1) Everyone has the right to education. Education shall be free, at least in the elementary and fundamental stages. Elementary education shall be compulsory. Technical and professional education shall be made generally available and higher education shall be equally accessible to all on the basis of merit.

(2) Education shall be directed to the full development of the human personality and to the strengthening of respect for human rights and fundamental freedoms. It shall promote understanding, tolerance and friendship

among all nations, racial or religious groups, and shall further the activities of the United Nations for the maintenance of peace.

(3) Parents have a prior right to choose the kind of education that shall be given to their children.

Article 27: (1) Everyone has the right freely to participate in the cultural life of the community, to enjoy the arts and to share in scientific advancement and its benefits.

(2) Everyone has the right to the protection of the moral and material interests resulting from any scientific, literary or artistic production of which he is the author.

Article 28: Everyone is entitled to a social and international order in which the rights and freedoms set forth in this Declaration can be fully realized.

Article 29: (1) Everyone has duties to the community in which alone the free and full development of his personality is possible.

(2) In the exercise of his rights and freedoms, everyone shall be subject only to such limitations as are determined by law solely for the purpose of securing due recognition and respect for the rights and freedoms of others and of meeting the just requirements of morality, public order and the general welfare in a democratic society.

(3) These rights and freedoms may in no case be exercised contrary to the purposes and principles of the United Nations.

Article 30: Nothing in this Declaration may be interpreted as implying for any State, group or person any right to engage in any activity or to perform any act aimed at the destruction of any of the rights and freedoms set forth herein.

SUMMARY OF THE CODE OF OFFENSES AGAINST THE PEACE AND SECURITY OF MANKIND

Not all law is made by formal enactment by a legislative body. The British Constitution is an excellent example of this non-legislative or common law.

The world common law is made up of the case law from international tribunals, consensus of nations as exemplified by the Charter of the United Nations, and generally agreed to principles as set forth in the Universal Declaration of Human Rights.

Of great significance to the body of the world common law is the work of the International Law Commission of the United Nations in drafting a *Code of Offenses Against the Peace and Security of Mankind* which was given substance by the Nuremburg and Tokyo trials of World War II. Even before the war-crime trials there existed considerable precedent to support a listing of the following acts as crimes against the world community.

A summary of the offenses enumerated in the Code:

Article I states that "Offenses against the peace and security of mankind are crimes under international law for which responsible individuals shall be punished."

Article II lists these offenses which are presented here in condensed form.

1. All acts of armed aggression.

2. Threats to resort to aggression.

3. Preparation, other than by authority of the United Nations, for the employment of armed forces against another state.

4. Incursion into the territory of another state of armed bands acting for political purposes.

5. The fomenting of civil strife in another state.

6. Encouraging terrorist activities in another state.

7. Violating treaty obligations designed to insure international peace and security.

8. Annexing territory belonging to another state.

9. Destroying or acting with intent to destroy, in whole or in part, a national, ethnical, racial or religious group.

10. Performing inhuman acts against any civilian population.

11. Acting in violation of the laws or customs of war.

12. Conspiring or inciting to any of these offenses.

Article III reads, "The fact that a person acted as Head of State or as responsible official does not relieve him of responsibility for committing any of the offenses defined in this code."

Article IV states, "The fact that a person charged with an offense defined in this Code acted pursuant to an order of his government or of a superior does not relieve him of responsibility in international law if in the circumstances at the time, it was possible for him not to comply with the order."

APPENDIX C

ACTIVITIES FOR PEACE

Here is a listing of some of the activities that have proven successful in spreading the spirit of world understanding and world co-operation among people.

1. Formation of a United Nations Week Committee in each town; this will take individual initiative as the mayor probably will not act without being requested to act.

2. The issuance of a United Nations Week Proclamation by the town or city mayor.

3. Have the governor of the state to issue a United Nations Week Proclamation, and to appoint a UN Week State Chairman in the early spring to insure sufficient time for the planning of an effective program. UN Week is in October of each year.

4. Have printed and distributed automobile bumper stickers. This is a most effective device for spreading a United Nations or world law message.

5. Contact the state restaurant association and have two United Nations or world law messages printed on one side of four by eleven cards so that as the cards are folded "tent fashion" they will stand erect when placed on a table with a message on either side. Each restaurant places these cards on their tables and the messages are then seen

by hundreds of thousands of persons as they patronize public eating establishments.

6. Work with your local garden club to have a world peace through world law or United Nations Week tree-planting ceremony. The trees and shrubs can be donated by your garden club and planted under their supervision by school children to commemorate the founding of the United Nations or to emphasize the need for a world peace under law.

7. Present to schools and local and state governments United Nations flags with appropriate ceremonies and press coverage.

8. Conduct United Nations Day flag raising ceremonies at which public officials gather and speeches are made on the theme of world peace through world law or on some phase of the United Nations and its work.

9. A United Nations parade when well planned and where sufficient resources and parade experience are available is a tremendously effective device for making the man in the street aware of the world-wide significance of the United Nations.

10. One of the very finest ways to raise monies for United Nations activities is through the sale of United Nations Cookbooks obtainable from UN Bookstore, UN Headquarters, New York 17, New York.

11. Suggest that local organizations have United Nations meals during UN week based on recipes gotten from the United Nations Cookbook.

12. Encourage merchant associations to give prizes for the best United Nations window displays during UN Week.

13. Be sure to include all young peoples' groups in United Nations Week activities; such groups as the Boy and Girl Scouts, Y-Teens should not be overlooked.

14. An art contest with two divisions, one for the children and one for adults, is a splendid project which has a wide appeal. It is suggested that a general theme; for example, "The UN in Building A Better World," be used.

15. Picnics, athletic contests and dances are good projects by which funds can be raised to defray the costs of peace activities.

16. County and state fair world law and United Nations booths from which informative materials are distributed have proven very effective.

17. Have a public address on world affairs. Often a speaker can be obtained without charge through contacting the consulates in Washington. It is best first to see if a speaker cannot be obtained through a local area United Nations speaker service. A nearby law school or college political science department can also be an excellent source for a good speaker.

18. Recordings and short films made for radio and television by famous actors describing the work of the UN and the need for world law can be obtained through peace organizations. (See direct membership organizations in Appendix D of this volume.)

19. Get some local manufacturer, group or individual to begin a United Nations and world law bookshelf in the local school library, having printed or typed and placed in each book an appropriate acknowledgment indicating the name of the donor.

20. School teachers should be provided film strips on world law and UN themes. These can be obtained through the UN Association of the U.S. (See Appendix D of this volume.)

21. Contests are interesting and effective means to attract attention to the United Nations. For example,

articles from various countries can be placed in a store window and the public asked to guess their national origins.

22. Have bulletin board displays in schools and churches regarding the UN and world law.

23. Have United Nations style show as a device to raise money for peace activities. Neither dresses nor models need be representative of the countries they honor.

24. Window displays in shop windows using posters, costumed dolls and colorful items from other countries directing attention to the activities of the United Nations.

25. Be sure all peace activities including topical studies by organizations are well and consistantly covered in the press even if this involves the hiring of a professional publicist or public relations man, even if this person can work only part time.

26. Order, distribute and display world law and United Nations materials to schools, churches, civic clubs and other groups. Materials can be obtained through the UN Association of the U.S. (See Appendix D of this volume.)

27. From time to time have current United Nations and world law material distributed to the public from a sidewalk booth which has been colorfully and attractively decorated. Materials can be obtained through UN Association for the U.S. (See Appendix D of this volume.)

28. Rent and show films dealing with world law and United Nations subjects to groups of all types. Write the U. S. Association for the UN. (See Appendix D of this volume.)

29. Contact the Advertising Council for professionally written copy advertising the United Nations and its work; these "spots" and "mats" are usually run without charge as a public service by mass communications media.

30. Obtain scripts for plays on a United Nations theme and suggest to local schools that they put on a United Nations play. (Write: U.S. Asso. for the U.N.; see Appendix D of this volume.)

31. In those larger cities where there is a symphony orchestra, have a program of music from various countries with the program appropriately dedicated to a better understanding between nations and peoples.

32. Purchase and use UNICEF Christmas and greeting cards. Write UN Bookstore, UN Headquarters, New York 17, New York.

33. Every town should participate in the UNICEF "Trick or Treat" programs whereby money is collected for the benefit of undernourished children throughout the world. (Write: UNICEF, UN Headquarters, New York City 17.)

34. Radio and TV discussions are excellent when informed participants are available.

35. By all means solicit the continuing interest of public officials in all United Nations projects.

36. Secure the services of able United Nations and world law speakers and create a speaker bureau making known to all local organizations that they can have a good speaker speaking on a United Nations or world law subject.

37. Form local councils on world affairs and ask each local organization to have a representative on this council.

38. Conduct United Nations study and speaking contests in every high school, sending the winner and his or her teacher to the United Nations for a few days to observe the UN in action. This program including the trip can be carried out at a nominal cost. This project can be financed and sponsored by a local organization as its inter-

national relations project. (Write: American Freedom Association. See Appendix D of this volume.)

39. A town can find great reward in sponsoring a community ambassador: a citizen to live with a family abroad for a period of time and return home to speak on his or her experiences and impressions to local organizations.

40. Encourage local pen-pal activity with citizens of other countries.

41. Do not restrict peace work to civic groups but be sure all religious faiths and other interested organizations are invited to participate and join in peace activities.

42. Suggest to ministers that they speak often of the need for world co-operation and organization to promote peace. Emphasize that as the followers of the Prince of Peace, ways to peace and brotherhood should be their chief concern throughout the year, not just on UN Week Sunday.

43. Reminders of the significance of the United Nations should appear in church bulletins during United Nations Week and at such other times as groups within the church undertake UN activities or world law studies.

44. Financially support all United Nations and world law affairs with as much money as you can afford.

45. By all means let your views on the need for world law be known to your Congressmen, Senators, the Secretary of State and the President.

46. Be a reader and learn all you can about international affairs, the UN and world law. (See Appendix E.)

47. Join with others in your effort to promote the United Nations and world rule of law. (See Appendix D.)

48. Personally speak out for the United Nations and a governed world under just law.

49. December 10th of each year marks the anniversary of the Declaration of Human Rights. This great document came into being in 1948 and it is most fitting that every year this anniversary be observed in every city and town.

MAJOR PEACE ORGANIZATIONS

American Baptist Convention
Council on Christian Social Progress
152 Madison Avenue
New York 16, New York

*American Freedom Association
World Peace High School Speaking Program
Corriher Avenue
Salisbury, North Carolina

American Friends Service Committee
160 North 15th Street
Philadelphia 2, Pennsylvania

Carnegie Endowment for International Peace
United Nations Plaza at 46th Street
New York 17, New York

Catholic Association for International Peace
1312 Massachusetts Avenue, N.W.
Washington 5, D. C.

*Major direct membership organizations

Center for Research on Conflict Resolution
820 East Washington
University of Michigan
Ann Arbor, Michigan

Central Committee for Conscientious Objectors
2006 Walnut Street
Philadelphia 3, Pennsylvania

Commission on Justice and Peace
Central Conference of American Rabbis
136 Seventh Avenue, North
Nashville 3, Tennessee

Committee for Application of Behavioral Sciences
To Strategies of Peace
(ABSSOP), P. O. Box 5926
San Francisco, California

Committee For Nonviolent Action
325 Lafayette Street
New York 12, New York

Committee for World Development and World Dis-
    armament
218 East 18th Street
New York 3, New York

Committee on National and International Affairs
American Psychological Association
1333 Sixteenth Street, N.W.
Washington 6, D. C.

Congress of Scientists on Survival (SOS)
21 Washington Place
New York 3, New York

Council for a Livable World
Dupont Circle Building
1346 Connecticut Avenue, N.W.
Washington 6, D. C.

Council for Correspondence
Emerson Hall 324
Harvard University
Cambridge 38, Massachusetts

Council for the Gradualist Way to Peace
c/o Dr. Amitai Etzioni, Sociology Department
Columbia University
New York, New York

Division of Peace and World Order
Methodist Board of Christian Social Concerns
100 Maryland Avenue, N.W.
Washington 2, D. C.

Federation of American Scientists
1700 K Street, N.W.
Washington 6, D. C.

Fellowship of Reconciliation
Box 271
Nyack, New York

Five Year Meeting of Friends
Board on Peace and Social Concerns
101 Quaker Hill Drive
Richmond, Indiana

Foreign Policy Association
345 East 46th Street
New York 17, New York

Friends Committee on National Legislation
245 Second Street, N.W.
Washington 2, D. C.

Friends General Conference
Peace and Social Order Committee
1515 Cherry Street
Philadelphia 2, Pennsylvania

Friends Peace Committee
Philadelphia Yearly Meeting
1520 Race Street
Philadelphia 2, Pennsylvania

General Strike for Peace
63 West 14th Street
New York 11, New York

International Confederation for Disarmament and Peace
5 Caledonian Road
London, England

Institute for International Order
11 West 42nd Street
New York 36, New York

Institute for International Studies
Box 538, Lone Pine Road
Chapel Hill, North Carolina

Mennonite Central Committee
Akron, Pennsylvania

Methodist Board of World Peace
740 Rush Street
Chicago 11, Illinois

National Committee for a Sane Nuclear Policy (SANE)
17 East 45th Street
New York 17, New York
Legislative Office; 245 Second Street, N.E.,
Washington 2, D. C.

National Council on Industrial Growth and Conversion
130 East 59th Street
Room 900
New York 22, New York

National Service Board for Religious Objectors
401 Third Street, N. W.
Washington 1, D. C.

Peace Action Center
1731 Park Road, N. W.
Washington 10, D. C.

Peacemaker Movement
10208 Sylvan Avenue (Gana),
Cincinnati 41, Ohio

Peace-Politics Clearing House
44 Brattle Street
Cambridge 38, Massachusetts

Peace Research and Education Project
715 Arch Street
Ann Arbor, Michigan

Peace Research Institute
1329 18th Street, N.W.
Washington 36, D. C.

People-to-People
2401 Grand Avenue
Kansas City 8, Missouri

Platform for Peace
1314 NE 43rd Street
Seattle 5, Washington

Political Action for Peace (PAX)
56 Boylston Street
Cambridge 38, Massachusetts

Society for Social Responsibility in Science
Gambier, Ohio

Student Peace Union
6029 University Avenue
Chicago 37, Illinois

Students for a Democratic Society
112 East 19th Street
New York 3, New York

Tocsin
E-32 Dunster
Harvard University
Cambridge, Massachusetts

Turn Toward Peace
Box 401
Cooper Station
New York 3, New York

United Christian Missionary Society
Disciples of Christ
Department of Social Welfare
222 South Downey Avenue
Indianapolis 7, Indiana

*United Nations Association of the United States
345 East 46th Street
New York 17, New York

*United World Federalists, Inc.
1321 14th Street, N.W.
Washington 5, D. C.

University Committee on Problems of War and Peace
c/o Professor Otto Feinstein
Wayne State University
Detroit, Michigan

War Resisters League
5 Beekman Street
New York 38, New York

Women's International League for Peace and Freedom
2006 Walnut Street
Philadelphia 3, Pennsylvania

Women Strike for Peace
1822 Massachusetts Avenue, N.W.
Washington 6, D. C.

*World Association of World Federalists
Burgemeester Patijniaan 49
The Hague
Netherlands

World Peace Broadcasting Foundation
3005 High Street
Des Moines 12, Iowa

*Major direct membership organizations

World Peace Foundation
40 Mt. Vernon Street
Boston, Massachusetts

World Peace Through Law Center
400 Hill Building
Washington, D. C.

World Rule of Law Center
Duke University
Durham, North Carolina

PEACE PUBLICATIONS

Bulletin of the Atomic Scientists
    434 S. Wabash Avenue
    Chicago 5, Illinois, $6 per year, monthly

Council for Correspondence Newsletter
    Council for Correspondence
    Emerson Hall 324
    Harvard University
    Cambridge 38, Massachusetts, $6 per year, monthly

Foreign Affairs
    Council on Foreign Relations
    58 East 68th Street
    New York 21, New York, $6 per year, quarterly

I. F. Stone's Biweekly
    5618 Nebraska Avenue, N.W.
    Washington 15, D. C., $5 per year, biweekly

Intercom
    Foreign Policy Association
    345 East 46th Street
    New York 17, New York, $.75 per copy, $5 per year

International Organization
  World Peace Foundation
  40 Mt. Vernon
  Boston 8, Massachusetts, $5 per year, quarterly

Journal of Arms Control
  Institute for Arms Control and Peace Research
  Box 1106
  Ann Arbor, Michigan, $7.50 per year, quarterly

Journal of Conflict Resolution
  University of Chicago Press
  5750 Ellis Avenue
  Chicago 37, Illinois, $5.50 per year, quarterly

Liberation
  110 Christopher Street
  New York 14, New York, $4 per year, monthly

War/Peace Report
  305 West 18th Street
  New York 11, New York, $5 per year, $3.50 for
    students, monthly

World Politics
  Woodrow Wilson Hall
  Princeton, New Jersey, $6 per year, quarterly